The Big Bands Songbook

The Big Bands Songbook

Compilation and text by George T. Simon

BARNES & NOBLE BOOKS
A DIVISION OF HARPER & ROW, PUBLISHERS
New York, Cambridge,
Philadelphia, San Francisco, London,
Mexico City, São Paulo, Sydney

Music Autography by Irwin Rabinowitz and Saul Honigman

This work was originally published by Thomas Y. Crowell Company.

THE BIG BANDS SONGBOOK. Written text copyright © 1975 by George T. Simon. All rights reserved. Printed in the United States of America. No part of this book may be used or reproduced in any manner whatsoever without written permission except in the case of brief quotations embodied in critical articles and reviews. For information address Harper & Row, Publishers, Inc., 10 East 53rd Street, New York, N.Y. 10022.

First BARNES & NOBLE BOOKS edition published 1981.

LIBRARY OF CONGRESS CATALOGUE CARD NUMBER: 84-48054

ISBN: 0-06-464049-3

90 13

Introduction

I was flattered and somewhat surprised when George Simon asked me to write an introduction to this book. In the first place, though my band and I were fortunate enough to have been in the right place at the right time, and so were able to contribute to the big band era, I have never considered myself an authority on the pop songs of the thirties and forties, or, for that matter, of any other era. In the second place, as I look through this collection of songs, I am reminded that, though we did have some fine tunes in those days, this book, which I recognize covers more than just the music of the swing bands, contains a certain number of songs which I did not like then, have subsequently forgotten, and, frankly speaking, am not remotely tempted to add to my repertoire. But, of course, that is purely a matter of personal taste, and I hasten to add that there are also many songs in this book that I have always enjoyed enormously, both to play and to listen to.

I am pleased to see that George has done his usual wonderful job of writing and research. I must commend him also for having chosen the songs most closely associated with the various bands. His stories and anecdotes are both informative and amusing, and I am sure that they will evoke many memories for the readers who danced or listened to these bands in those days.

As for those who were not there, this book, I believe, should give them an excellent insight into the music, the spirit, and the over-all feeling of the big bands. Many of these songs may already sound familiar, because through the past thirty years they have been played and sung all over the world, and quite a number of them have even become classics and therefore a part of American folklore.

This book has many uses. You can sing to it. You can play to it. Or you can use it simply as a wonderful vehicle for reminiscing and evoking the sounds and spirit of a period that was very dear to us, including a very grateful clarinet player named

BENNY GOODMAN

Preface

They were exciting years—those years of the big bands—when for less than a buck you could spend an entire evening watching and listening to the music of your favorite orchestras in ballrooms and theaters or, for several quarters more, in hotel supper rooms and roadhouses and even at your college prom.

On the other hand, if you just wanted to listen without looking, you could tune them in almost any time of day or night—live or on records—on just about every radio station in America. Or else, if you wanted their music on a more permanent basis, you could go to your local record shop and there, in a little glass-enclosed booth, audition any one of the dozens of those breakable, seventy-eight r.p.m. records that came out each week, buying only those you liked and returning the rest to your local, friendly, disappointed record clerk. And chances are, he'd never hassle you, either!

For those were different, far less pressured times. Relationships were more simple, more direct, more trusting and a lot more naive. The complexities and the suspicions that emerged after World War II, when the pace of living increased so drastically, when competition became so very much more intense, and when, more and more, motives began to be questioned (and perhaps rightfully so), gave rise to an entirely different attitude toward life and its values and the basic precepts of human relationships.

Perhaps nothing reflects these changes more dramatically than a comparison of some of the music of today with that of the big bands, one and a half to two generations ago. Much of today's music is assertive, strident, forceful, often very self-conscious and concerned with projecting a social message. (And, when one considers the state of the world these days, such emphasis is understandable.)

On the other hand, the music of the more relaxed, less competitive big band era, though seldom projecting the sort of intensity, strength or social concerns that today's songs do, reveals instead a simplicity and charm and, in its own way, a quiet reassurance that reflected rather well a less-questioning, more-accepting way of life.

The majority of the songs of the big band era, including those that covered the war years, appealed to simple emotions, mostly love, and very sentimental love at that. The structures of the songs, too, were comparatively simple and predictable, and so was the way singers related to their audiences.

Theirs was a "me-to-you" approach, with no complex gimmicks, like over-dubbing, reverb chambers and other electronic gadgets, to becloud what was willingly accepted as a very personal message from a very special performer.

The nearness between band singers and fans was often more than merely a feeling: It could also be quite physical. During the big band days, no super-stars strutted behind overpowering arrays of security guards with blaring speakers to keep the fans from coming too close. Sure, there were idols, like Glenn Miller and Frank Sinatra and Benny Goodman and Gene Krupa, but they were approachable. If you arrived at a dance early enough, you could stand right in front of your idols, or maybe even right next to them. You could talk with them. You could even touch them. And invariably you would feel that their music was coming directly, right there, from them to you—as indeed it was—instead of being created electronically and often too mechanically through a whole series of purely impersonal gadgets.

As I started to say, those were exciting times. The fans would line up dozens deep around a bandstand, calling for their favorite songs or singers or musicians. And they knew what they were calling for, too. They knew who was playing what in which band, and they followed their favorites just the way sports fans have always followed their pet players. When a band would come to town to play a theater, their followers would often line up hours before opening time, and then sit through some second- or third-rate movie several times just so they could see and hear their band on successive stage shows.

And, of course, they knew which bands played the most attractive versions of which songs. In those days, often the same songs were played and sung by numerous artists. Most of them were written not by the performers themselves, but by professional songwriters for music publishers, who would then contact either the performers or the record companies to get them to play their songs. Sometimes the bands could create a hit simply by playing a song often enough on their radio broadcasts. More often, however, hits were made as they still are today: through phonograph records.

Here again, the routines during the big band era were far less complicated. Instead of taking weeks and relying on sixteen-track monster recording machines to complete a few sides, the big bands often recorded four of theirs in just three hours. It was simply a matter of blowing their music into a few mikes, and then letting the record company reproduce their creative efforts. And because no recording gimmicks were involved, the bands could recreate in person precisely what they had put into the recorded grooves, and don't think that the kids didn't clamor for those hits whenever a band came to their town for a personal appearance!

Of course, *how* the band treated those songs was crucial. Here the arrangers, usually working closely with the leaders, played important interpretive roles. And so, of course, did the band vocalists, for the way they sang a song could often be the deciding factor in turning it into a hit or a miss.

This book is concerned with seventy-plus of the biggest of those hits and how they happened to get that way. Its purpose is threefold: (1) to make it

possible for you to play and sing some of the big song hits of the big bands;
(2) to let you know what was going on inside those bands—what the leaders
and the singers and the musicians were really like; and (3) to tell you something about each of these songs and to show you how important they were to
the successes of so many of the big bands.

In putting this book together, I again contacted many of the leaders and
singers and composers and publishers with whom I had established close and
warm relationships during the big band days. To all of those who cooperated
so beautifully with me on this project—the performers and the composers, as
well as the music publishers, without whose aid I could never have assembled
all these seventy-plus great songs—I offer my deepest gratitude. I would also
like to thank Benny Goodman, the catalyst and the predominating force in
getting the whole big band era started, for his gracious introduction; Nick
Ellison, my editor, who has a wonderful way of giving an author his head,
while helping him meet those elusive deadlines; Irwin Rabinowitz and Saul
Honigman, who did such a handsome job of autographing the music; Bob
Asen and Milt Lichtenstein of *Metronome* magazine; Chuck Suber of *Down
Beat* and Columbia Records for their cooperation in assembling the photos;
and, once again, my wife, Beverly, who worked so gently, graciously, reassur-
ingly and effectively helping to prepare a book that I hope will bring back
many wonderful memories to those of you to whom the music of big bands
remains something special, and much enlightenment and an equal amount
of pleasure to those who hadn't yet arrived, but who now would like to know
what it was really like then.

GEORGE T. SIMON

Stamford, Conn.
May 1975

[viii]

Contents

♪♪♪

[x]

Ain't Misbehavin'

♪♪♪

He wrote "Ain't Misbehavin' " in forty-five minutes. He wrote parts of "Honeysuckle Rose" while he was talking on the telephone. And he composed portions of a major Broadway musical, *Hot Chocolates,* on stage with chorus girls rehearsing numbers all around him.

There was a lot to go around him, too, for Fats Waller was a huge man, with a talent to match. One of the great jazz pianists of the ages, a warm and witty entertainer, he was also an outstanding composer.

Thomas "Fats" Waller came from a musical family. His father was a violinist; like her son, his mother sang, and played both piano and organ. Thus, it's not surprising that when he was still very young, Fats began performing and composing, and that he wrote his first hit song, "Squeeze Me," with Spencer Williams, when he was only fourteen years old. From then on he proceeded to compose a whole slew of hits, including "Honeysuckle Rose," "I've Got a Feeling I'm Falling," "Keepin' Out of Mischief Now," "My Fate Is in Your Hands," "Jitterbug Waltz," which was the first jazz tune in 3/4 time, "Stealin' Apples," which became Benny Goodman's favorite instrumental, "Changes," "Blue Turning Gray Over You," and two songs from *Hot Chocolates:* (1) "Ain't Misbehavin'," one of the most popular tunes of all time, and (2) a song whose lyrics, accepted at first, were resented for years as overtly racial, and only recently, because of semantical revisions, have been accepted: "(What Did I Do to Be So) Black and Blue." And he also wrote the scores for two more Broadway musicals, *Keep Shufflin'* in 1929, and *Early to Bed* in 1943, the year in which he died.

Though he led a big band for only a short period, Waller was definitely an imposing, impressive and influential figure on the big band scene. His tunes, simple, direct, musically correct and fetchingly rhythmic, were played by almost all the big bands, sweet as well as swing, and he was, of course, as comments regarding the song "I'm Gonna Sit Right Down and Write Myself a Letter" show (see page 151), a man of extraordinary performing talents.

The slightly misbehavin' Mr. Waller.

Ain't Misbehavin'

Lyric by ANDY RAZAF
Music by THOMAS WALLER and HARRY BROOKS

Slowly, with expression

No one to talk with, all by my-self,
No one to walk with, but I'm hap-py on___ the shelf, Ain't mis-be-hav-in',
I'm sav-in' my love for you.___

And the Angels Sing

ঐ ঐ ঐ

"It was Ziggy Elman who brought that number in to us," Benny Goodman recalls, referring to one of the three great trumpeters (Harry James and Chris Griffin were the other two) who sparked his band in the late thirties. "He had recorded it as an instrumental with his own little group on the Bluebird label, and when it started to become a hit, I asked Johnny Mercer to write some lyrics for it. It was originally a Hebrew folk tune, you know, and Ziggy had done it as a *frälich*—in fact, part of his solo on our record is in *frälich* tempo—the rest, of course, is in straight 4/4 time, just like any other pop song."

"And the Angels Sing" turned out to be one of the most joyous-sounding records of the swing era. In addition to Ziggy's trumpet, it featured a delightful vocal chorus by Martha Tilton—"Liltin' Martha Tilton" they used to call her—a darling petite blonde whom Benny had plucked out of the Three Hits and a Miss vocal group that was singing on his 1938 radio commercial series. The kids loved her, and so did the guys in the band. After she left Goodman in the spring of 1939, she embarked on a successful radio career, and today still sings occasionally—and as charmingly as ever, too!

Ziggy—his real name was Harry Finkelman—had been featured with Alex Bartha's band on Atlantic City's Steel Pier when in the summer of 1936 Goodman discovered him. He was a brilliant trumpeter, whose fat, schmaltzy sound had a strong influence on the ballad playing of Harry James. Benny remembers Elman not only as "a terrific first trumpeter" but also as "a very sweet guy, who worked like hell. He had a great sense of humor and was very understanding, and you had to like the guy." Eventually, Ziggy joined Tommy Dorsey's band, with whom he was also featured, then settled in the West Coast studios. But ill health pursued him and in June 1968 his horn was stilled forever.

"And the Angels Sing" remains as a monument to Ziggy, and also as one of the Goodman band's all-time hits. In many ways it reflects ideally the happy, free-swinging spirit that made the swing era such a special time for those lucky enough to have participated in it.

Singing angel Martha Tilton and Benny Goodman.

Goodman and Elman at a 1950's reunion.

And the Angels Sing

Lyric by JOHNNY MERCER
Music by ZIGGY ELMAN

A-Tisket, A-Tasket

♩♩♩

Van Alexander, who wrote "A-Tisket, A-Tasket" with Ella Fitzgerald, still remembers well how it all happened back in 1938:

"Ella was with Chick Webb's band and they were playing at a place called Levaggi's up in Boston. I was the band's arranger, and that meant that each week Chick would give me three arrangements to do, and after I'd finished them, I'd take the train to Boston, pick up three more assignments, go home to New York to write them and then return the next week.

"One day Ella said to me, 'I have an idea for doing something with an old nursery rhyme.' And she asked me if I'd work out something with her on 'A-Tisket, A-Tasket.' I told her 'Sure,' but Chick kept feeding me so many new songs to arrange that I kept neglecting her. Finally she said, 'Look, you've never done anything with that song,' and so the next week I sat down and wrote out the arrangement."

Alexander, who today is a successful conductor-arranger in Hollywood's TV studios (he was Dean Martin's musical director for some years), contributed the middle part (the release) to enlarge the nursery rhyme into a standard thirty-two-bar pop tune. "I wrote some extra lyrics, but Ella kept on improving them. For example, I'd written 'walkin' on down the avenue,' but she changed it to 'truckin' on down the avenue.' I remember we rehearsed it one afternoon just before a radio broadcast, and we were even making lyric changes then. That night Chick and Ella did it on the air, and it was almost an immediate hit. Maybe that's how hit songs are made, on the spot like that, instead of slaving over them for months."

"A-Tisket, A-Tasket" became Chick's and Ella's biggest number. Unfortunately, little Chick, the dynamic hunchback, the idol of Gene Krupa and other top drummers, lingered only a year or so after his record became a top-seller. When he died in 1939, Ella fronted the band, but a few years later she gave up her leader's role and embarked on her fabulously successful solo career.

Van Alexander still sees her occasionally. So do others of us who remember her as the shy but exuberant kid singer on the bandstand of the Savoy Ballroom, standing by the side of the brass section, making little motions as she followed the band's various riffs, forever anxious to get up front to do her vocals.

Ella with Chick (lower left corner) at the drums.

"Yes, she was a shy girl then; she still is today," Van recently remarked. "But she remains as sweet and as gracious as always." And—even though it may be coming out of her ears by now, close to two generations later—she still sings "A-Tisket, A-Tasket" wherever she goes. "If that's what you want," she tells her huge, enthusiastic audiences all over the world, "that's what you're going to get," as she swings into her song without the slightest hint that maybe she wishes, just for one night at least, she could really "lose her little yellow basket"!

A-Tisket, A-Tasket

Words and Music by ELLA FITZGERALD
and VAN ALEXANDER

Basin Street Blues

♩♩♩

"Glenn Miller came into the recording studio that day, and he had a whole verse, words and everything, all arranged for 'Basin Street Blues,' " recalls Charlie Teagarden, Jack's younger, trumpet-playing brother, who also played on the Charleston Chasers' memorable 1931 recording session that jazz historians still rate as one of the era's greatest. Benny Goodman had organized the group, but the highlight of "Basin Street Blues" turned out to be Jack Teagarden's singing and trombone playing of the song with which he was to be associated for the rest of his life.

"That whole portion—you know, 'Won't you come along with me, down the Mississippi'—Glenn had worked out before the date," stated Charlie from Las Vegas, where he is now a leading musicians' union official. "He was such a talented man!"

Goodman remembers the session and Miller the same way. He and Glenn had been close friends ever since the mid-twenties when both had joined Ben Pollack's band, in which Teagarden later replaced Miller because he could play better jazz trombone. But Glenn, always the complete gentleman, showed no resentment. Instead, he worked closely with Jack on numerous recording dates, sometimes playing trombone at his side, other times writing arrangements of tunes like "The Sheik of Araby," "After You've Gone," "Beale Street Blues" and "Basin Street Blues," all successful jazz recordings, and all featuring Teagarden's singing and trombone.

The main portion of "Basin Street Blues" had been written by one of the best, most productive and most overlooked of the early jazz composers. He was Spencer Williams, a college-educated black from Louisiana (a rarity at the turn of the century), who as far back as 1916 had written "I Ain't Got Nobody" and had followed it with such jazz staples as "Everybody Loves My Baby," "I've Found a New Baby," "Royal Garden Blues," "Shim-Me-Sha-Wabble," "Mahogany Hall Stomp" and "I Ain't Gonna Give Nobody None o' This Jelly Roll," the last two made famous by Louis Armstrong and Bessie Smith respectively.

More than any other number, "Basin Street Blues" established Jack Teagarden as the greatest of all jazz trombonists. In 1933 he joined Paul Whiteman's band, where he was featured for five years; then in 1939 he started his own big band, a rich-sounding, quasi-dixieland outfit built around

"Won't you come along with me?"

Jack's singing and trombone and Charlie Spivak's brilliant lead trumpet.

After the end of the big band era, Jack, as warm in person as he sounded on his trombone, led several small jazz groups, then became an important voice and more or less alter ego in Louis Armstrong's greatest All Stars, which time and again sparkled with his ageless singing and playing of "Basin Street Blues."

Basin Street Blues

by SPENCER WILLIAMS

Won't-cha come a-long with me, To the Mis-sis-sip-pi?

We'll take a boat__ to the lan' of dreams,__

Steam down the riv - er down to New Or - leans;__ The band's there to meet us,

Beat Me, Daddy, Eight to the Bar

♩♩♩

The Will Bradley band had two leaders and two styles. Up front stood Will, a handsome man, who played pretty ballads on his trombone. In back sat Ray McKinley, a scholarly-looking drummer with a wild imagination, who sometimes sang and who was featured, along with pianist Freddie Slack, on a series of big band boogie-woogie arrangements.

Will and Ray had been friends for years. They had played together in the early thirties; then each had gone his separate way, Bradley becoming one of New York's top studio musicians (Glenn Miller referred to him as "the best in the business"), and McKinley the featured drummer in Jimmy Dorsey's band. When they reunited in 1939 to form their band, they weren't exactly sure in which musical direction they were going—pretty music, swing, or what.

Then Ray hit upon big band boogie-woogie. The eight-to-the-bar driving jazz style, based on the standard twelve-bar blues progressions, was the big musical fad at the time, but it was being played almost exclusively on the piano by specialists like Meade Lux Lewis, Albert Ammons and Pete Johnson. "Freddie and Leonard Whitney—he was our arranger—and I used to wonder what boogie-woogie would sound like by a big band," McKinley recalls. "So we got Leonard to write a few boogie-woogie arrangements.

"Well, one night we were playing one of them down at the Famous Door on Fifty-second Street. There was one part in the arrangement where I had a drum break, but for some reason or other that night, instead of *playing* the break, I *sang* out, 'Oh, Beat Me, Daddy, Eight to the Bar.' "

It so happened that a couple of astute songwriters named Don Raye and Hughie Prince were in that club that night, and they called McKinley over to their table and asked him if they could write a song using the "break" that McKinley had sung. Ray said "Sure"; they wrote the song; the Bradley band, with Ray singing and Slack playing boogie-woogie piano, recorded it, and it became their biggest hit. Naturally, they tried the same formula again and again—"Scrub Me, Mamma, with a Boogie Beat," "Bounce Me, Brother, with a Solid Four," and "Fry Me, Cookie, with a Can of Lard"—but none ever attained the popularity of "B.M.D.8T.T.B."

McKinley later led his own band, as well as Glenn Miller's AAF and civilian outfits after the Major's disappearance. He still migrates from his home in

Slack, Bradley and McKinley in eight-to-the-bar.

Bradley, McKinley and Slack long after eight in some bar.

Stamford, Connecticut, to front jazz groups. Sometimes an extra-hip jazz fan will ask him to "sing the song about Peck Kelley," the legendary Texas pianist. "They seem to think that line in 'Beat Me, Daddy' about 'a little honky-tonky village in Texas, there's a guy who plays the best piano by far' refers to Peck. But it doesn't. I had no special town and no special pianist in mind, though some years later Peck did thank me for the plug. But really, it was just my imagination running wild—just the way it did the night I decided to sing the break instead of playing it. Maybe, if I'd kept my dumb mouth shut we'd never have had that hit!"

Beat Me, Daddy, Eight to the Bar

Words and Music by DON RAYE, HUGHIE PRINCE
and ELEANOR SHEEHY

But the style he likes the best is eight to the bar; When he plays it's a

ball, He's the dad-dy of them all._____

Chorus

The peo-ple gath-er a-round when he gets on the stand,

mp - mf

then when he plays he gets a hand. The

Beer Barrel Polka

♩♩♩

Ever hear of Jaromir Vejvoda, Wladimir A. Timm and Vasek Zeman? They're three of the writers of one of America's most popular all-time hits. Americans? No. They're Czechoslovakians, and in 1934 they wrote "Skoda Lasky," which became a big hit in their country and in Germany. And how many Americans ever heard of "Skoda Lasky"? Very few, if any—that is until 1939, when Wladimir A. Timm changed its title to "Beer Barrel Polka" and Lew Brown, a veteran Tin Pan Alley lyricist, wrote the famous "Roll out the barrel" lyrics.

Another question: Who is Will Glahi? He's the leader of the orchestra that waxed the first American hit version of the song for RCA Victor and which by now has sold millions of copies. All sorts of groups and singers have been recording the song ever since, including Bobby Vinton, who in 1975 made still another hit version.

"We'll have a barrel of fun!"

At about the time that "Skoda Lasky" was becoming Americanized, a young North Dakota bandleader with a thick European accent was beginning to make quite a name for himself in Chicago's Aragon and Trianon ballrooms. His eleven-piece band, once known as the Hotsy Totsy Boys, had already begun, under the guidance of its accordion-playing leader, to develop its Champagne Music style. And one of the first sides that Lawrence Welk recorded, on the Vocalion label, and which helped greatly to bring him and his band into national prominence, was "Beer Barrel Polka."

Few bandleaders have remained as dedicated as Welk to their principles and their public. Recognizing both the talents of others as well as his own limitations, he has kept his music simple and his gracious smile in evidence. "You have to show a little friendliness, let's say it that way, and you do the things you know you can do." Responding recently to a rather unfavorable review of his band in 1941, in which he was at least given credit for "pleasant accordion interludes," he commented modestly and accurately, "Far more pleasant are those by Myron Floren," his current accordionist.

Probably more than any other bandleader, Welk has kept alive the sounds of the big bands through his tremendously successful network and syndicated television shows. Responding to "those New York, Chicago and Hollywood" types who would have him deviate from his musical and business philosophies, he states unequivocally, "My years of one-nighters in small towns throughout the country taught me what the people want." And he has been giving it to them ever since, while they, in turn, have been giving him what he wants: their appreciation and admiration and, one suspects, at least a million or more bucks.

Beer Barrel Polka

Words and Music by LEW BROWN, WLADIMIR
A. TIMM, VASEK ZEMAN and JAROMIR VEJVODA

Fast Fox Trot *(like a polka)*

There's a gar‑den, what a gar‑den, On‑ly hap‑py fa‑ces bloom there And there's nev‑er an‑y room there For a wor‑ry or a gloom there Oh! there's mu‑sic and there's danc‑ing And a lot of sweet ro‑

Boo-Hoo

♩♩♩♩

Guy Lombardo has always been recognized as the leader of the Guy Lombardo Orchestra, and rightfully so. For it was always his business acumen and his organizational and administrative ability, all blended with an amazingly consistent intuition for giving the public what it wanted, that contributed so much to his band's success.

But behind the scenes, brother Carmen played an especially important role. He was recognized as the band's musical director, and his conceptions, along with his distinctive, wavering vibrato both on saxophone and tonsils, helped give the band its unique, easily recognizable sound.

Carmen was both well-liked and respected. In addition to playing, singing and often rehearsing the band, he wrote hit songs, including "Coquette" and "Sweethearts on Parade," which he composed back in 1928, and "Snuggled on Your Shoulder," "A Sailboat in the Moonlight," "Seems Like Old Times" and "Boo-Hoo," which he wrote in 1937 in collaboration with John Jacob Loeb and one of the era's finest and most prolific lyricists, Eddie Heyman ("Body and Soul," "Out of Nowhere," "I Cover the Waterfront," "You Oughta Be in Pictures," "Bluebird of Happiness" and many more).

The Lombardo band's rendition of "Boo-Hoo" typified its stylized approach. In addition to the wheezing saxes, it utilized the clipped, muted brass, the almost inaudible rhythm section, and the vocal trio, led by Carmen's tantalizing tremolo.

In analyzing his band's success, Guy has always given his brother much credit. "Carmen's vibrato," he once explained, "always had a lot of soul." Then, stressing the importance of a musical identity, he stated, "The big trick, when you're doing a radio broadcast, is to be recognized without an announcer telling you who it is."

That wasn't always such an easy trick to pull off, however, because once the Lombardo band had achieved its astounding success, others began imitating it, not always well, to be sure, but closely enough to raise some doubts. But the one thing nobody—not even those who poked fun at him—could duplicate was Carmen's singing, whether as a soloist or as leader of the vocal trio featured on a succession of big Lombardo hits, including, of course, "Boo-Hoo."

The Lombardo brothers: Lebert, Carmen, Guy and Victor.

The Lombardo band: Guy with the fiddle; Carmen at his right elbow.

Boo-Hoo

Words and Music by EDWARD HEYMAN,
CARMEN LOMBARDO and JOHN JACOB LOEB

Chattanooga Choo-Choo

♪♪♪

"All I know is that we had to write something for Glenn Miller for his first movie, *Sun Valley Serenade,* so we sat down and wrote 'Chattanooga Choo-Choo,' " said eminently successful, eighty-two-year-old and still very chipper Harry Warren on the phone from his Beverly Hills home. "That's the way we used to do things in those days [the early forties]. Mack [Gordon] and I were writing songs for one picture after another. I wish I could tell you there was something romantic connected with each of them, but, really, there wasn't. We just had a job to do, and we did it. Actually, I worked more like a tailor: I wrote songs to suit the occasion or the band."

"Chattanooga Choo-Choo" fit the Miller band so well that it became the first million-record seller since Gene Austin's "My Blue Heaven," issued fifteen years earlier. To honor this achievement, RCA Victor presented Glenn with a gold-plated copy of his record, and this became the prototype of the Gold Records now awarded by the Record Industry Association of America for all million-sellers.

In *Sun Valley Serenade,* a good deal of "Chattanooga" footage was devoted to the Nicholas Brothers dancing a typical Hollywood routine to the song. On the recording, however, the emphasis was solely on Glenn and his vocal-

"Hi, there, Texas, what'cha say?"

"Pardon me, boy, is that the Chattanooga Choo-Choo?" Marion Hutton with (left to right) Modernaires Bill Conway, Ralph Brewster, Hal Dickenson and Chuck Goldstein, and Tex Beneke, Ray Eberle and Glenn Miller.

ists, Tex Beneke, Marion Hutton and the Modernaires, singing together, a mixture obviously very attractive to record buyers.

Glenn, a perceptive arranger and producer, knew exactly how best to. utilize his vocalists' technical limitations. By her own admission, Marion was a better entertainer than singer (one of Miller's sidemen once observed dryly during one of her lesser successes, "The mike sure is out-of-tune tonight"). But she possessed an infectious, girl-next-door personality, and Glenn wisely assigned her roles that projected her assets rather than her liabilities.

As for Beneke, he had never sung with a band before joining Miller's, yet Glenn had such an intuitive ear for talent that at Tex's first rehearsal with the band, Miller suggested he try singing. Tex turned out to be one of the era's most popular singers, a warm, down-home personality, who also played lovely ballads on his tenor saxophone, but whose relaxed, lightly swinging "Aw-shucks-I'm-really-not-that-good" vocals became an even stronger commercial asset for the band.

The Modernaires, four lads from Buffalo, New York, also lent important voices to the band, especially on rhythm tunes like "Chattanooga Choo-Choo." They had joined Glenn specifically to record "Make-Believe Ballroom Time," a new theme for New York's top-rated all-night radio show, and made such an impression on Miller and his fans that Ralph Brewster, Bill Conway, Hal Dickenson and Chuck Goldstein immediately became Miller regulars.

After Glenn disbanded in September 1942 to accept a commission in the army, and Tex went into the navy, Marion made a few movies, then retired to raise a family. However the Mods, despite numerous personnel changes, kept on singing for years, while Tex, after his return from the service, led the official Glenn Miller band from January 1946 to December 1950. He still surfaces with various pickup groups, never failing, of course, to fulfill his fans' demands to take them on yet another trip on the Chattanooga Choo-Choo.

Chattanooga Choo-Choo

Lyric by MACK GORDON
Music by HARRY WARREN

Cherokee

ᏜᏜᏜ

The biggest hit record of "Cherokee," composed by Ray Noble, who led one of the prettiest *sweet* bands of all time, was created by two of the *swingingest* cats on the big band scene, bandleader Charlie Barnet and arranger Billy May.

Noble had originally written the tune as part of an *Indian Suite,* a serious work of several sections, each dedicated to a different American Indian tribe. Actually, Count Basie's band was the first to recognize the lovely tune's swingability in February 1939 with its two-sided lightly swinging version. Then a few months later, Billy May, a young trumpeter and arranger who had just joined the Barnet band, was so knocked out by that Basie record that one night while riding the Barnet band bus, he knocked out an even more jumping arrangement. This one featured a classic, roaring tenor sax solo by Barnet himself, and created such a furor that Charlie decided to use the tune as his theme song.

Barnet could roar and create furors even without his tenor sax. An extremely handsome man, grandson of a New York Central Railroad vice-president, and a Yale dropout, Barnet projected the carefree good times that many associate with the big band era. His band was always swinging and loose, just like its leader, who was constantly uncovering and encouraging new talent.

Most famous of all his discoveries was a pretty young Cotton Club dancer turned singer. Her name: Lena Horne. And he featured other talented black artists with his band, long before such a blend was generally acceptable—trumpeters Peanuts Holland, Al Killian and Clark Terry, trombonist Trummy Young and bassist John Kirby. Doc Severinsen, for years leader of the band on television's "Tonight Show," also got his start with Barnet. So did famed arrangers Neal Hefti and Ralph Burns. So did singers Kay Starr, Fran Warren and Frances Wayne.

Ask just about anyone who ever worked in Charlie Barnet's band, and you'll hear them all say the same thing: It was one big ball. But it was a great musical experience, too. For, though Charlie encouraged and respected good musicianship, he hardly ever interfered with the spontaneous attitudes

Charlie Barnet greets his idol, Duke Ellington.

of the men and women who worked—no, the word really should be "played"—for him, either in their musical or in their personal lives.

Few bandleaders can boast such a long list of illustrious and grateful graduates.

Cherokee

Words and Music by
RAY NOBLE

Ciribiribin

♩♩♩

"Let me tell you how I happened to choose 'Ciribiribin' for a theme song," Harry James was saying in the winter of 1975 over the phone from Florida, where his band was on still another string of personal appearances. "I was with Benny's [Benny Goodman's] band and Benny wanted Ziggy [Elman] and me to be featured on a special solo each. Ziggy chose 'And the Angels Sing,' but I couldn't figure out what to pick. So one night George Koenig, my roommate, suggested 'Ciribiribin.' Now, as you know, that was originally an old Italian folk song, and it had always been played just the way it was written—as a waltz. And that's how I always played the first chorus, too. But from then on it was different. Both George and I could see that the tune lent itself perfectly to a virtuoso performance, with a strong, swinging beat going on behind it. So that's how I did it."

James left Goodman late in 1938, having gained little recognition for his rendition of "Ciribiribin," though Elman's "And the Angels Sing" had become a big hit. However, after he formed his own band a few months later, Harry decided that his version of the old folk song would supply just the kind of flash opening that could identify his band, which in those days leaned heavily toward high swinging arrangements built around Harry's horn.

He recorded it twice. The first version was strictly instrumental, featuring Harry's schmaltzy open trumpet playing the melody just straight and then going off into a romping, roaring finish. "But then Frank [Sinatra] joined the band, and they asked us to record it again, this time with Frank singing both the verse and the chorus." The result was a two-thirds, one-third ratio for Sinatra over James—an interesting record but not typical of the way Harry treated the old folk song, nor one of Sinatra's better efforts, by any means.

Perhaps the most memorable of all the James renditions of the tune occurred in September 1942, during Glenn Miller's final Chesterfield radio show from the stage of the Central Theater in Passaic, New Jersey. Spotted in the Miller arrangement of "Juke Box Saturday Night" were sixteen bars of "Ciribiribin," with Miller's trumpeter, Johnny Best, doing a takeoff on James. But on this special program, right in the middle of the arrangement, just before Best was ready to blow, out onto the stage strode James himself to perform a truly dramatic presentation of "Ciribiribin."

[53]

Harry.

The 1939 James band: Harry flanked by singers Connie Haines and Frank Sinatra.

Of course there was a reason for this. The following week, with Miller having gone into service, the Harry James band took over the Chesterfield series, and for a long time thereafter reigned as the country's number-one dance band.

Ciribiribin

Music by A. PESTALOZZA
Arranged by HARRY JAMES
Lyrics by JACK LAWRENCE

Moderato *(Swingy)*

Ci-ri-bi-ri-bin He waits for her each night be-neath her bal-co-ny _____ Ci-ri-bi-ri-bin He begs to hold her tight but no she _____ won't a-gree_

Cow-Cow Boogie

By 1942, boogie-woogie had become so well established that its songwriters tried looking for various gimmicks on which to hang different versions of the twelve-bar blues phrase. Two of the music's more prolific composers were Gene DePaul and Don Raye, and in what appears to have been one of the more peculiar musical gap-bridging bits, they decided to try combining some of the elements of jazz with some of the philosophies of country music.

The result was "Cow-Cow Boogie," a tale of a hip cowboy, which they brought to the attention of Freddie Slack, who had been specializing in commercial boogie-woogie piano (he had been featured with Will Bradley's band), and who had recently organized his own band and had landed a recording date with then-brand-new Capitol Records.

Freddie needed a pretty hip singer for this tune, preferably one who could also sound like somebody "from down Texas way." Some years previously, Slack had played piano in Jimmy Dorsey's band. Its vocalist for a short time had been an attractive Texas lass named Ella Mae Morse, who lasted with the band only a month—just long enough, apparently, to have made a lasting impression on Slack.

Ella Mae Morse surrounded by Olsen and Johnson, with young Mel Torme at the drums in a scene from *The Ghost Catchers*.

Ella Mae might have stayed longer with the Dorsey band had she not been so young and inexperienced. She did possess a swinging beat, an earthy, vital way of phrasing and an apparent penchant for problems. On one broadcast she unwittingly sang some very risqué network-banned lyrics instead of the approved set; on another she completely forgot the words of the song she was singing. Her naiveté could be quite charming, as her co-vocalist, Bob Eberly, once noted. "The night she forgot those words, she just smiled sweetly at the mike, and then right on the air turned to Jimmy and said something like, 'My, I forgot the words. Now isn't that just awful? I don't know what to do.'" But Dorsey did. He let her go.

The Slack-Morse combination made a big hit out of "Cow-Cow Boogie," one of Capitol's very first releases and the Slack band's first and last really successful recording. It also launched the fast-maturing Ella Mae on a highly successful career that eventually led to her own long-term recording contracts and numerous nightclub and television appearances. As for Slack, he kept on playing his boogie-woogie role, which he admitted he really didn't enjoy at all, eventually working mostly in small clubs on the West Coast, until the middle of 1965 when he passed away.

Cow-Cow Boogie

Words and Music by DON RAYE, GENE DE PAUL
and BENNY CARTER

"swing half - breed"___ Sing-in' his Cow-cow Boog-ie___ in the

strang -est way___ "Cum-a-ti-yi-yi ay, Cum-a-ti-

yip - it-tl-e-yi-ay"___ Tsk Tsk

Tsk Tsk Yip pee e e e e e. . . .

(8)

Daddy

♩ ♩ ♩

"It was Sammy Kaye's record of 'Daddy' that opened up a whole new world for me," Bobby Troup was saying in his sumptuous Encino, California, home, which he shares with his wife, Julie London, and their children, and which they sometimes leave to travel to the TV studios to play their leading parts in the "Emergency" series.

"I wrote the song in 1940 at the University of Pennsylvania for the freshman Mask and Wig Show, and it became popular around the campus. Some nights I'd hang around the Embassy Club, an after-hours spot in Philadelphia, where show people came in after work, and sometimes I'd even play the piano. There was this group there called the Kurt Weil Quintet, and they heard 'Daddy' and asked me if I'd mind if they made an arrangement of it. Of course I was flattered, and every once in a while Kurt would tell me that so-and-so had come into the club and had liked my song.

"Well, one night—it must have been around eleven o'clock or even later—Kurt called me at the house and said to come down right away, that Sammy Kaye had heard the song five times and wanted to talk to me. So down I went and met Sammy, and he told me he'd like to do my song. Now, I was so green then, I would have sold it to him for seventy-five bucks. But Sammy was a very honorable man, and he called his lawyer, Lee Eastman, in New York right then and asked him to send down a contract for the song. I signed it, and later found out that it was a very, very fair contract.

"Sammy began playing the song on his 'Sunday Serenade' radio series, and he recorded it too, and it wan't long before it made the Hit Parade. It stayed there for seventeen weeks, and in the number-one spot for seven of them. And you know what? Sammy and his arranger, 'Pump' Handle—how's that for a name for you?—used almost exactly the same arrangement that Kurt Weil had been playing in the club."

As Troup said, "Daddy" did open up a whole new world for him. He had been attending the Wharton School of Finance at the University of Pennsylvania, and had been elected to the Beta Gamma Sigma fraternity, which is the Phi Beta Kappa of the business schools, winding up with the third highest average in his large class. But the success of "Daddy" so encouraged him ("The first thing I did was to go out and buy two Buicks—one for myself and one for my mother!") that Bobby took his songwriting career seriously, com-

"Daddy, I want a diamond ring . . . !"

posing, among other tunes, "Route 66," "Baby, Baby, All the Time," "Snooty Little Cutie" and "Girl Talk." He also sang and played on records, encouraged and coached his future wife, Julie London, and hosted his own musical series on both radio and television—and all because of "Daddy."

Daddy

Words and Music by
BOB TROUP

Deep Purple

When Larry Clinton started his band late in 1937, he was all set to have one of the swingingest outfits around. But one traumatic experience thwarted that ambition. Let him tell about it:

"We were playing a battle of music at the Green Key Ball at Dartmouth College. Jimmie Lunceford's was the other band. We were there bright and early, but Jimmie, who was supposed to go on first, didn't arrive until just a few minutes before he was to play. So he asked me if I'd mind opening the dance while his men got washed up.

"Well, we played about an hour, and I trotted out all our flag-wavers. Then Jimmie came on, and after he'd played just a minute or so of 'For Dancers Only,' with the great beat his band had and the trumpets tossing their horns in the air and everything, I made up my mind right then and there that I could play nothing but sweet things if I was going to survive that night. Maybe that's why I began to concentrate on pretty things from then on."

The experience turned out to be a bonanza for Clinton. He did begin to concentrate more on ballads, which his band played very tastefully and which, he found, contrasted effectively with his fewer swing numbers.

Many of the ballads featured a warm, sensuous singer named Bea Wain, whom Larry heard singing "just eight bars on a radio show. She was then a member of Kay Thompson's Choir. I knew immediately that she was what I wanted for my band." Hers was an important voice on two of the band's biggest sellers, Clinton's adaptation of a Debussy theme which he called "My Reverie" and the Mitchell Parish–Peter DeRose collaboration on "Deep Purple."

Parish recalls that the melody was extracted from an instrumental suite that DeRose, a highly gifted composer, had written for the Paul Whiteman orchestra. "In those days, many of us worked directly for music publishers. Peter and I were both with Mills Music. Often we would gather together in the late afternoons and exchange ideas. And it was at one of those sessions that Peter asked me to write lyrics for his theme."

"Deep Purple" became a huge hit, and helped to elevate Bea Wain into one of the era's top singing spots: a star of the "Lucky Strike Hit Parade" series. Subsequently she was featured on numerous other radio shows; then,

The Larry Clinton band in the Terrace Room of the Hotel New Yorker. Bea Wain is at the mike.

after her marriage to famed radio announcer André Baruch, she went into semi-retirement. Eventually they moved to Florida, where for years they hosted a top-rated radio talk show.

Clinton also moved to Florida. A man of many talents (he was a top flyer during the war), he became a successful writer, not of music but of fiction and nonfiction, and with his wife of more than forty years he now leads one of the most serene lives of any of the big band leaders.

Deep Purple

Lyric by MITCHELL PARISH
Music by PETER DE ROSE

Slowly (*with feeling*)

When the deep pur-ple falls o-ver sleep-y gar-den walls, and the stars be-gin to flick-er in the sky,_____ Thru the mist of a

The Dipsy Doodle

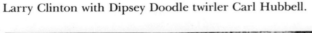

In addition to some of the pretty ballads that Larry Clinton turned out with those lovely vocals by Bea Wain, he continued to dabble in swing tunes. Before organizing his band in 1937, he had written novel jazz arrangements for the Dorsey Brothers Orchestra, then for Jimmy Dorsey, then for Glen Gray and the Casa Loma Orchestra, and finally for Tommy Dorsey's band.

His forte was composing light, descriptive, semi-swinging instrumentals, like "Tap Dancers' Nightmare," "Dusk in Upper Sandusky," and "Satan Takes a Holiday." Then, shortly before forming his own band, he wrote the biggest of all his instrumental hits, "The Dipsy Doodle."

"I remember I was sitting in the old Onyx Club on Fifty-second street. It was the musicians' hangout and they had menus with blank music staves on

Larry Clinton with Dipsey Doodle twirler Carl Hubbell.

them. While I was waiting for some of my friends from the Casa Loma band to come in, this riff came to me, and so I jotted it down on the menu.

"It was sort of a wacky-sounding thing and it needed a wacky-sounding title. Then I remembered Carl Hubbell of the Giants and the screwball pitch he used to throw. They called it the dipsy-doodle pitch, so that's what I called my new tune."

Tommy Dorsey had recently recorded Clinton's "Satan Takes a Holiday," and it had become a hit, so it seemed the perfectly natural thing for him to take his newest song to Tommy, who liked it and immediately recorded it. Shortly thereafter, Larry organized his band. By then "The Dipsy Doodle" had become a hit, so naturally he used it as his identifying theme. But he faced one problem: Both Tommy and he were recording for the same label, RCA Victor; Tommy's recording had already been established, and neither he nor the record company was about to release a competing version on the same label. So, poor Larry couldn't even record his own theme!

But Larry really didn't care that much. Tommy's record paid off handsomely with royalties, and even if Larry couldn't record his own tune, he could and did play it on many, many live radio broadcasts from top spots throughout the country from 1938 to 1941, until he broke up his band to accept a commission as a flying captain in the United States Air Corps.

The Dipsy Doodle

Words and Music
by LARRY CLINTON

Swingy

The Dip-sy Doo-dle's a thing to be-ware.

The Dip-sy Doo-dle will get in your hair. And if it gets you it

could-n't be worse, The things you say will come out in re-verse, like:

Don't Sit Under the Apple Tree

♩♩♩

The Andrews Sisters introduced one of the wartime's most popular and most wishful-thinking songs, "Don't Sit Under the Apple Tree," in a 1942 film, *Private Buckaroo,* that also presented the Harry James band. It was a year during which name bands continued to be starred and featured in Hollywood's movies. Glenn Miller, between filming *Sun Valley Serenade* and *Orchestra Wives,* recorded another popular and even more swinging version of "Don't Sit Under the Apple Tree," complete with lots of singing by Tex Beneke, Marion Hutton and the Modernaires.

Soaring attendance figures in movie houses that also featured stage shows must have convinced Hollywood moguls of the big bands' popularity. Thus, during that one year, they hired Harry James, Kay Kyser and Skinnay Ennis to make two movies apiece. Xavier Cugat, Jimmy Dorsey, Tommy Dorsey, Sonny Dunham, Woody Herman, Sammy Kaye, Freddy Martin, Ozzie Nelson, Ray Noble, Harry Owens, Phil Spitalny and others also appeared in full-length films with their bands. And in one movie, *Syncopation,* seven leaders—Harry James, Benny Goodman, Charlie Barnet, Gene Krupa, Joe Venuti, Alvino Rey and Jack Jenney—all participated in an exciting all-out jam session.

The Andrews Sisters, easily the most popular girl singing trio of the big band era, went the bands one better that year: in addition to *Private Buckaroo* they made two more movies, *Give Out, Sister* and *What's Cookin',* in which they were joined by Woody Herman's band. Two years earlier they had been starred with Glenn Miller, not in a movie, but on a thirteen-week radio series for Chesterfield cigarettes. At the time, the sponsors weren't sure that Miller's band was well known enough to retain an audience, so for the opening weeks they included the sisters on the program. But once the response had determined the tremendous extent of Miller's popularity (then, as now, sponsors and advertising agencies needed constant reassurance), Patti, Maxene and LaVerne departed the show and continued their fabulously successful personal-appearance tours.

"Don't Sit Under the Apple Tree" proved to be custom-made for its times, when boys were away from their girls, wondering what they were doing, with girls, back home, wondering just as much what their boys were doing, and each group avidly hoping that the other would heed the original words of Charlie Tobias not to "sit under the apple tree," and especially Lew Brown's follow-up line of "with anyone else but me."

Maxene, Patti and Laverne Andrews and Glenn.

"Don't sit under the apple tree with anyone else but me!"

Don't Sit Under the Apple Tree (with Anyone Else but Me)

Words and Music by LEW BROWN, CHARLIE TOBIAS
and SAM H. STEPT

Elmer's Tune

♩♩♩

"There was this fellow named Elmer Albrecht, who was an undertaker's assistant who used to work right near the Aragon Ballroom in Chicago where we were playing," bandleader Dick Jurgens was saying over the phone from his home in Sacramento, California. "He played a little piano, and Andrew Karzas, who owned the ballroom, used to let him come in every day at noon, when nobody was in the place, to practice.

"Well, I used to come over sometimes around noon to work with a secretary and answer all our fan mail, and I used to hear Elmer playing his little warm-up ditty—it was only about four bars or so—but it got to me. I remember the chords were exactly like 'If I Could Be with You One Hour Tonight.' So one day I got together with Elmer and I finished the song for him.

"Now, Elmer used to come into the Aragon fairly often, so as a surprise for him we scratched out an arrangement, and whenever he'd come into the place we'd play it for him. Well, don't you know, it began to catch on with the customers, and they started requesting 'Elmer's Tune.' And so then we began playing it on the air.

"One day I got a call from Glenn Miller. He said, 'Hey, Dick, what's all this about "Elmer's Tune" that I've been hearing about?' And I told him the story, and he said he'd like to record it. He'd only heard it as an instrumental, the way we were playing it on the air, so he asked me if it had any words. I told him 'No,' but I'd have some written. So I immediately called a songwriter I knew in Chicago, Sammy Gallop, and asked him to come right out to the Aragon. About half an hour later there he was. He had been hearing the tune on the air and had thought about writing some lyrics to it, but he couldn't quite figure out how you could write words to something called 'Elmer's Tune.' Anyway, I gave him a lead sheet and told him to give it a try. Well, don't you know that less than an hour later he called me on the phone, and he read me the lyrics. And they were so good that we never changed a single word!"

Both Miller and Jurgens made hit records of the tune. Glenn's featured Ray Eberle and the Modernaires, while Dick's, recorded before the lyrics had been written, focused on Lew Quadling, his pianist. Both records sold over a million copies, and the song remained on the Hit Parade for seventeen consecutive weeks.

Maestro Jurgens.

Sometime later, Elmer Albrecht and Dick Jurgens teamed up for an encore. They called it "Elmer Does It Again." But Elmer didn't, and so back in his mortuary he was forced to settle for dreams of greatness and royalties from just one tune.

Elmer's Tune

Words and Music by ELMER ALBRECHT, SAMMY
GALLOP and DICK JURGENS

Moderately *(with rhythm)*

Why are the stars al - ways wink - in' and blink - in' a - bove? What makes a fel - low start think - in' of fall - in' in love? It's not the sea - son, the rea - son is

Good Night Sweetheart

The song that ends more dances and brings more partners closer together than any other is a lovely ballad written by the leader of one of the finest orchestras ever to glow on the big band scene.

Ray Noble wrote "Good Night Sweetheart" in 1931, when he was still home in England. There he had led a magnificent orchestra, composed of the country's top musicians whom he assembled in the HMV (His Master's Voice) recording studios for regular dates. The results so impressed American band bookers Rockwell-O'Keefe that they decided to bring Noble to the States, not realizing (1) that he really had no set band and (2) that the musicians' union wouldn't have stood for such an importation anyway. And so, when they found out what they couldn't do, they went ahead and did what they could do. They engaged Glenn Miller, who had played such an important role in forming the Dorsey Brothers orchestra, to organize a band of American musicians for Noble.

It turned out to be one of the finest bands of all time, including in its roster future bandleaders like Miller, Charlie Spivak, Claude Thornhill and Will Bradley, as well as outstanding sidemen like Bud Freeman, Johnny Mince, Peewee Erwin and George Van Eps. Its first and most important engagement in 1935 was in Radio City's recently opened Rainbow Room, a very swank spot which required formal dress, and where the orchestra played seven nights a week until three in the morning.

Among the tunes it featured were such lovely Noble compositions as "The Very Thought of You," "By the Fireside," "Love Is the Sweetest Thing," "Love Locked Out" and, naturally, "Good Night Sweetheart." Noble not only wrote, but also arranged these numbers, which, like all the band's ballads, were performed with consummate good taste.

But the band also had a swinging side, and that's where Miller took over, providing semi-dixieland arrangements of jazz tunes that would set off its talented soloists.

The Noble-Miller mixture worked well for about a year. But both men possessed strong personalities, and their growing disagreements became more profound and disruptive. Miller and others began to depart, and Noble, a very bright, articulate gent, who had been educated at Cambridge, concentrated more on commercial radio. He moved to California, where he

The Ray Noble band in the Rainbow Room. Horns in back row: trombonists Glenn Miller and Will Bradley; trumpeters Charlie Spivak and Peewee Erwin. Pianist is Claude Thornhill; saxist at far right is Bud Freeman.

became musical director and a delightful stooge on the Edgar Bergen series. He formed another band and continued to write more hit songs—"The Touch of Your Lips," "I Hadn't Anyone Till You" and "Cherokee"—then returned to England for a spell, finally coming back to America in 1970 to settle down in Santa Barbara, California.

Good Night Sweetheart

Words and Music by RAY NOBLE, JIMMY
CAMPBELL and REG CONNELLY

Goody Goody

There seems to be much agreement among those who were there in 1935 that the catalyst for the launching of the big band craze was Benny Goodman. When his band appeared at the Palomar Ballroom in Los Angeles that summer, the place seemed to explode, so powerful was the dancers' reaction, and particles from that explosion soon spread to cities and towns all over America.

This was a tremendous band, built around Goodman's fiery clarinet; tightly knit, swinging arrangements by Fletcher Henderson, Jimmy Mundy, Edgar Sampson and others, and featuring such brilliant sidemen as drummer Gene Krupa, trumpeter Bunny Berigan, pianist Jess Stacy and, later on, of course, trumpeters Harry James and Ziggy Elman, pianist Teddy Wilson and vibraphonist Lionel Hampton.

During the course of an evening most swing bands often settled into non-rhythmic ruts as they acceded to dancers' requests to play at least a few recognizable pop tunes in addition to their swinging instrumentals. Not so Goodman's, however, because its playing of pop tunes also featured a swinging beat. And during those first years, even during vocal choruses, the beat never slackened, because Helen Ward, a very pretty, sexy-looking lass, imbued everything she sang with intense rhythmic excitement.

One of Helen's best and most requested numbers was "Goody Goody," a tune constructed so rhythmically that it could almost swing itself. "Believe it or not," Helen recently admitted from her Virginia home, "I hated that thing the first time I heard it. I almost cried. But after a while I began to love it. And you know I always adored working with Benny!"

"Goody Goody" was one of Johnny Mercer's earlier songs. As Johnny remembers it: "Matty Malneck [its co-writer] and I were still with Paul Whiteman's band [Malneck was a violinist; Mercer a vocalist], and between sets at the Biltmore Hotel we used to sit down and write songs. Benny was a good friend, and after he started his band I played some of my songs for him. The first one he recorded was 'The Dixieland Band.' Helen sang that one too. Then came 'Goody Goody.' On the strength of its popularity, we got a contract writing for the movies.

"I will say this for Benny: He believed in me long before the others did. I'll always be grateful to him." And so will millions of others, not because he

BENNY GOODMAN'S
SATIONAL SWING BAND
TALK OF THE MUSIC WORLD

The 1936 Goodman band in Chicago's Congress Hotel. Helen Ward is the singer, Gene Krupa the drummer.

Master lyricist Mercer; masticator Goodman.

performed their songs, but because Benny Goodman, despite a couple of discouraging years, believed strongly enough in big band swing to stick it out, until he found his believers that night at the Palomar, and for at least forty more years thereafter.

Goody Goody

Words and Music by JOHNNY MERCER
and MATT MALNECK

So you met some-one who set you back on your heels, good-y good-y! So you met some-one and now you know how it feels, good-y good-y! So you gave him your heart too just as

Got a Date with an Angel

♩♩♩

"It was a tune that I especially liked. It was written by some Englishmen, you know, and I heard it for the first time when I was over in England with the Hal Kemp band in 1930. I had become quite an Anglophile by then. Maybe if I hadn't, I might have sat down and written some songs myself and made some money."

The speaker is John Scott Trotter, who played piano and arranged for the Hal Kemp band, and who created its unique musical style. One of its focal points was its singing drummer, Skinnay Ennis, born Robert Ennis in the state of North Carolina, where he had attended the University at Chapel Hill and linked up with Kemp and his band.

"The moment I heard the song, I knew it would be ideal for Skinnay," Trotter continues. "So after we came back, and we were playing at the William Penn Hotel in Pittsburgh, I sat down and wrote out the arrangement." It became Kemp's biggest hit.

Ennis had a unique, shy, breathless singing style that captivated many of his female listeners. A quiet man, with a soft, thick, southern accent, he had by 1938 achieved enough fame with Kemp to go out on his own. He took over a West Coast band led by Gil Evans, then a very young arranger, and

Skinnay.

Hal.

engaged Claude Thornhill, who was still to form his own band, as pianist, arranger and musical director. It was a good band, and naturally it used "Got a Date with an Angel" as its theme song. Ennis by then was colorful and popular enough to attract the attention of Bob Hope, who hired him for his top-rated radio series as band leader, singer and part-foil and part-comedian.

Skinnay also played parts in the movies—in *Sleepy Time Gal, Swing It, Soldier,* and *Follow the Band*. During the war, he led a service band, then rejoined Hope on his radio show, and was leading a relaxed life and career until his death in the early sixties. As one sage pointed out, "Few singers ever entertained more people with less breath!"

Got a Date with an Angel

Words by CLIFFORD GREY and SONNIE MILLER
Music by JACK WALLER and JOSEPH TUNBRIDGE

Heartaches

♪♪♪

If you're going to be absolutely literal about the big hit records of the big bands, "Heartaches" shouldn't have any lyrics printed along with the music. For the record that brought fame to Ted Weems in the autumn of his life didn't even have a vocal chorus. Instead, it featured a guy named Elmo Tanner. And what did Elmo do? He just whistled.

He was quite some whistler, Elmo was, and Ted Weems was quite an astute and very much loved bandleader. His was never one of the greatest musical outfits; instead it concentrated more on entertaining the dancers with a nice, homey, personal approach. To accomplish this, Weems, a warm, jovial man, featured in addition to his whistler, half a dozen singers, among them a handsome Crosby-like crooner with a shock of black, wavy hair, who stayed with Weems for six years. His name: Perry Como. Also featured were Marvell Maxwell, who later changed her name to Marilyn Maxwell and became a

Weems and young vocalist Como.

movie star, and a comedian named Red Ingle, whose later recording of "Timtayshun," featuring Jo Stafford, turned out to be a big hit.

According to Como, "The band was really built around its singers. I can't recall that it ever played a straight instrumental." As for Weems himself: "Ted was a good businessman and a gentleman in every sense of the word— in his actions and in his dress and everything. I don't think the man had a mean bone in his body."

As for his recording of "Heartaches," that took fourteen years to become a hit. Weems had introduced the song during a 1933 radio broadcast from a Chicago hotel. "We played it just the way it sounds on the record, with that corny sort of half-rumba rhythm and the whistling and all those effects. After the broadcast, the writers and the publisher called me on the phone, and they really let me have it. They claimed I was ruining their song."

But the public didn't agree. The recording became moderately successful. Then, in 1947, a disc jockey in North Carolina latched on to the old recording, complete with Elmo Tanner's whistling, and just kept playing it over and over again. His listeners were enthralled, and soon the word spread to other disc jockeys throughout the land. Naturally, they wanted to see what would happen. So they tried the same experiment and got the same reaction, and so, fourteen years after he had first introduced the song, just when he was about ready to call it quits, Ted Weems had himself his biggest hit record.

Heartaches

Words by JOHN KLENNER
Music by AL HOFFMAN

Heart and Soul

One of the most popular and oft-played tunes for pianists of all types, amateur as well as professional, has been "Heart and Soul," one of the few collaborative efforts of two of the greatest songwriters, Hoagy Carmichael and Frank Loesser. And perhaps the most memorable rendition came from a pianist who, as a stylish bandleader and gentleman, was considered to be very professional, but, as a first-rate pianist, a bit more on the amateur side.

He was Eddy Duchin, an extremely handsome, likeable man and a superb showman. What he lacked in musicianship he more than made up for with the heart and soul he invariably put into all of his performances. Always elegantly dressed, often in white tie and tails, he gave the impression not only of owning every piano on which he played but also of having a deep-seated love affair with it. Swaying back and forth, and weaving from side to side, he would seemingly coax romantic passages from its keys via his highly stylized versions of tunes like "Heart and Soul" and others which he helped turn into hits. As one of his veteran sidemen once noted, "Many people

Maestro Duchin.

didn't *listen* to him as much as they *looked* at him. I'll say this for the man: He was the only musician I've ever known who could play a thirty-two-bar solo with thirty-two mistakes and get an ovation for it afterwards."

Duchin, a very smart and well educated man, had started out as a pianist in Leo Reisman's orchestra, one of the most popular of the late twenties and early thirties. Recognizing Duchin's appeal, Reisman began featuring him, and a few years later Eddy took over as leader at New York's Central Park Casino, the prestigious room that had been Reisman territory for many years.

The Duchin band continued to play the country's poshest spots, always supplying pleasant if never too exciting music. Though Eddy's technical lack of musical knowledge sometimes made it a bit difficult for him to communicate well with his men, his good looks, natural charm and excellent manners made it easy for him to mix with society's bluer bloods.

Duchin also traveled abroad, first as a bandleader, then as a lieutenant in the United States Navy. Following the war, he concentrated more on radio appearances, as failing health began to curtail his activities. In 1951, he died of leukemia. Several years later, Tyrone Power played the lead in Hollywood's projection of *The Eddy Duchin Story* with a performance that observers agreed did project rather elegantly both Duchin's heart and soul.

Heart and Soul

by FRANK LOESSER
and HOAGY CARMICHAEL

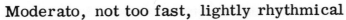

Moderato, not too fast, lightly rhythmical

I Can't Get Started

Bunny Berigan, one of the greatest trumpeters of all time and one of the most ineffective bandleaders, used this great Vernon Duke melody as the theme for his on-again, off-again, but definitely Berigan band. It certainly suited his musical style; its title also reflected very well his career as a band-leader. While his good friends Tommy and Jimmy Dorsey, Benny Goodman, Artie Shaw and Glenn Miller reached the top with their bands, poor Bunny never really could get started with his.

Berigan recorded "I Can't Get Started" twice: first a very personal sounding rendition with a small group for Vocalion Records, then his famous version—issued in both ten-inch and twelve-inch records—on RCA Victor. Lyricist Ira Gershwin, referring to the Berigan version as "a sort of classic in its field," credits it for the song gaining worldwide popularity.

"I Can't Get Started" first appeared in the Ziegfeld Follies of 1936. Know

Bunny.

who sang it to whom? Bob Hope to Eve Arden! The lyrics were totally topical then, but as the years went by, they began to sound dated. So Ira Gershwin began writing new, updated lines for special singers and special occasions. The originals are printed herewith, but there's nothing to stop you from doing what Ira has done for singers like Bing Crosby, Nancy Walker and Frank Sinatra: Have a ball by making up your own *au courant* lyrics.

Berigan's singing style has been faulted by some. But never his trumpeting! Few instrumentalists have made such an impact upon the jazz world (he was featured with Benny Goodman and Tommy Dorsey before starting his own band), and had he taken better care of himself and not succumbed in 1942 to pneumonia, brought on by too much high living, his fame might have been even greater.

But his recording of "I Can't Get Started," which in 1975 became one of the first ten recordings to be voted into the Recording Academy's Hall of Fame, has brought immortality to the song and to Bunny himself.

(P.S. Vernon Duke wrote the song several years before he brought it to Ira Gershwin. Its original title was "Face the Music with Me," but as Gershwin reported, "Nothing had happened to that version." But once Ira, and then Bunny, got ahold of it—wow!!)

I Can't Get Started

Words by IRA GERSHWIN
Music by VERNON DUKE

I Don't Want to Set the World on Fire

♪♪♪

"It was the summer of 1941 and we were playing in Asbury Park, New Jersey," recalls Tommy Tucker, now professor emeritus of music at Monmouth College, also in New Jersey. "We had heard that over in Philadelphia there was a big hit called 'I Don't Want to Set the World on Fire' that some singer was doing especially well. So Joe Galkin, our manager, decided to go over and find out what was going on. And you know who the singer was who was doing the song? It was the great Bon Bon, who had just left Jan Savitt's band and had come back to Philadelphia."

Galkin and Tucker contacted the song's publisher in New York, hoping to be the first to record the tune. But another band, Harlan Leonard and His Rockets, had already done so. "They played it at an up tempo," Tommy recollects. "But to me it seemed to sound better as a ballad."

On its next Okeh recording date, the Tucker band recorded "I Don't Want to Set the World on Fire" slowly and with feeling, and within a few weeks it had its first huge record hit. "And we almost didn't make it," Tucker ·remembers. "It was the fourth and final tune on the session, and our vocal trio was having a lot of trouble. But we finally did get it in, and, as you know, it was the biggest break our band ever had."

Like Lawrence Welk a North Dakotan, Tommy attended the University of

The young professor emeritus and singer Amy Arnell.

North Dakota, where he was elected to Phi Beta Kappa. He began his band-leading career there, eventually extending his baton into forty-seven more states. For years, his band featured two very good singers, Amy Arnell and Don Brown, and a lovely theme song, "I Love You, Oh How I Love You," written by Tucker.

One of the true gentlemen of the music business, Tommy came across as a gracious, genteel and rather reserved leader. His band played on both the Fibber McGee and Molly and the Georgie Jessel radio shows, as well as at some of the big bands' top spots. In 1960, Tucker started teaching at Monmouth College, where he became such a popular figure that after a short retirement he was reengaged, by popular demand, as professor emeritus. It couldn't have happened to a nicer gentleman.

I Don't Want to Set the World on Fire

Words and Music by EDDIE SEILER, SOL MARCUS,
BENNIE BENJAMIN and EDDIE DURHAM

I Don't Want to Walk
Without You

Helen Forrest, one of the finest of all band vocalists, had never been entirely happy singing in the bands of Artie Shaw and Benny Goodman. "I'll always be grateful to them," she recently said. "But," she admitted ruefully, "they had been featuring me more like they did a member of the band, almost like another instrumental soloist." Then along came her stint with James, and that was different. "Harry always gave me the right sort of arrangements and settings that fit a singer. It wasn't just a matter of my getting up, singing a chorus and sitting down again."

The earliest and possibly the most successful example of that "let's-give-the-girl-singer-a-break" format resulted in one of the band's biggest hits. On "I Don't Want to Walk Without You," Harry built his arrangement all around Helen, featuring her not merely on the main chorus but even on the verse, a rare and daring innovation.

"Harry loved that verse," recalls composer Jule Styne. "And of course it fit right in with the times—the guy gone off to war and the girl waiting for him back home."

"We'd just had our first big hit record of 'You Made Me Love You,'" James reports, "and for the first time songwriters were coming to us to dem-

Helen and Harry.

onstrate their songs, hoping, naturally, that we'd record them. I remember when Jule came to us with 'I Don't Want to Walk Without You.' He did it at a faster tempo than we played it, almost like a schottische. We slowed it down and that made a big difference."

"Sure Harry slowed it down," agrees Styne, who today has emerged as a top Broadway composer and producer. "He slowed it down so much that we were very upset. We couldn't see how anybody could hold those notes that long." Obviously he had underestimated Helen's breath control.

Harry and Helen recorded the song in mid-December of 1941. Three months later it had become so popular that it was voted the number-one spot on the prestigious Coca-Cola Spotlight Bands radio series. Previously, only Tommy Dorsey, Sammy Kaye, Freddy Martin and Glenn Miller had been sharing top honors, but Harry's "I Don't Want to Walk Without You" not only took over in March, but two months later was picked as the show's most popular record of all time. And, as per the verse's opening lines, song-pluggers and composers from all over began knocking on Harry's door, hoping he would create another huge hit—just for them.

I Don't Want to Walk Without You

by FRANK LOESSER
and JULE STYNE

Chorus

I Let a Song Go Out of My Heart

♩ ♩ ♩

Duke Ellington could have become a very discouraged gent after he had written "I Let a Song Go Out of My Heart" for one of the featured spots in the 1938 Cotton Club Show. It was a tune of which he was proud. But at the last minute it was withdrawn from the show and another Ellington piece, which really didn't mean much to Duke, called "Swingtime in Honolulu," was substituted only because it suited better the phony sort of floor-show drivel that appealed to many of the rich whites who'd go up to Harlem night spots to be entertained by the blacks.

But Duke was never a man who discouraged easily—if at all. Some years ago, during an interview, we touched on his philosophy. The matter of

The Duke points to saxist Johnny Hodges (left), featured soloist on "I Let a Song Go out of My Heart."

worrying arose. "Worry," he said, "is the shortcut to the end of the line. Nothing's worth worrying about because worrying destroys you." However, he added, though he refused to worry, he never refused to become concerned. "A man who's concerned," he explained, "is concerned about something he can do something about. He can solve a problem. But a man who worries can do nothing because worrying is purely negative. It eats, and it eats only you. It's completely destructive."

And so Duke worried not one iota about the deletion of "I Let a Song Go Out of My Heart" from the show. But he did become concerned—concerned enough to include it in some of his broadcasts from the Cotton Club. Benny Goodman heard it, and he started playing it. So did Red Norvo and Mildred Bailey. And soon the song that had been kicked out of the Cotton Club Show became one of the Duke's biggest hits.

Later that year, the Ellington band began an engagement at another Harlem spot, the Apollo Theater, whose clientele was more musically sophisticated than the Cotton Club's. So Duke decided to dress up "I Let a Song Go Out of My Heart" with a strong counter-melody. But the audience didn't react the way Duke had expected. It wanted the song without frills. So Duke canned his new counter-melody.

Once again he didn't worry. Using the same basic chords, he fashioned a complete piece out of his counter-melody and called it "Never No Lament." Strictly an instrumental, it appealed almost entirely to musicians and dyed-in-the-wool Ellington fans. So once more Duke took action. This time he asked Bob Russell, a young, aspiring lyricist, to add words to his counter-melody. Bob came up with "Don't Get Around Much Anymore," and the Duke had himself yet another huge song success.

By the way, those of you who feel so inclined, try having the pianist play "I Let a Song Go Out of My Heart" while you sing "Don't Get Around Much Anymore." Or switch them around. And don't worry: Either way you'll have yourselves one Ellington ball!

I Let a Song Go Out of My Heart

Words by IRVING MILLS, HENRY NEMO
and JOHN REDMOND
Music by DUKE ELLINGTON

I'll Never Smile Again

Did you know that the first big name band to record "I'll Never Smile Again" wasn't Tommy Dorsey? It was Glenn Miller, who recorded the tune in February of 1940, three months before Tommy did. But Glenn didn't have Frank Sinatra, and he didn't have the Pied Pipers and he didn't have Tommy's trombone, nor did he have Tommy's ability to get everyone into a truly relaxed mood. That's why the Dorsey rendition became a big hit and the Miller recording one of Glenn's most forgettable.

Tommy recorded his version in May of 1940, after some of the members of his band had met Ruth Lowe, an ex-pianist in Ina Ray Hutton's all-girl band, who had written the song in memory of her late husband. Like Tommy himself, a number of his fellow-workers were sentimentalists, and so they prevailed upon Dorsey to record the song.

At the session, Fred Stulce, a saxophonist in the band who also arranged and who was one of the fellows who had met Ruth Lowe, brought in his arrangement, a full-bodied, big band affair. But it just didn't seem to work out. So, after a few unsuccessful tries, Tommy, who had a great ear for creating warm moods, suggested to Sinatra and Jo Stafford and the Pied Pipers that instead of trying to treat this like a typical big band arrangement, they sing the song as though they'd just gathered around a piano late at night in somebody's house. He slowed down the tempo, and he had Joe Bushkin play delicately in the background on a celeste; he inserted a few bars of his own muted trombone; he used just a few accompaniment bars that Stulce had written for the reeds, and out came one of the most gorgeous, most mellow and most relaxed sides ever to grace the big band scene.

(For those of you who would like to try to recreate the Dorsey mood, we suggest you sing this song very softly and very slowly. And if you would like to split up the melody the way Sinatra and the Pied Pipers did, we have set the words that the whole group sang in regular roman type and those that Frank sang alone in italics.)

The Pied Pipers, Connie Haines and Frank Sinatra line up in back of the Tommy Dorsey band in a scene from *Las Vegas Nights*. Buddy Rich is the young drummer.

I'll Never Smile Again

Words and Music by
RUTH LOWE

I'm Gettin' Sentimental over You

One of the real "goose-pimple raisers" among swing era songs has always been Tommy Dorsey's lovely theme, "I'm Gettin' Sentimental over You." It featured Tommy's gorgeous trombone tone, blown so smoothly and so effortlessly that musicians would wonder whether he ever inhaled, as that soft, sensuous sound ushered in some of the big bands' greatest programs.

Few if any orchestras could match Tommy's for its all-around performance. It could do more things better than any band in the business. Its brilliant jazz numbers starred some of the era's great musicians: trumpeters Bunny Berigan, Peewee Erwin, Ziggy Elman and Charlie Shavers; drummers Davey Tough and Buddy Rich; pianist Joe Bushkin; tenor saxophonist Bud

A very sentimental gentleman.

Freeman; clarinetist Buddy DeFranco—just to name a few. And its warm ballads, in addition to Tommy's trombone, featured vocals by some of the era's greatest singers: Jack Leonard, Frank Sinatra, Jo Stafford and the Pied Pipers—just to name a few more.

They used to call Tommy "The Sentimental Gentleman of Swing," though by reputation he was far from a sentimentalist. Instead, he was known to have been a pretty hard-nosed, hard-driving tyrant, who demanded and usually got the most from all those who worked with and for him. But beneath that dynamic and, by the way, often very witty exterior there was, as those of us who had been privileged to get close to him discovered, a warm, very gentle and often very sentimental streak. If any of his friends, for example, ever needed anything, Tommy would be right there, with no questions asked. He was also a lavish and gracious host and gift giver. And there were times, too, when he'd let his hair down completely. He'd make it plain that he abhorred phoniness of any sort. And he even confessed to me one time that his biggest hangup of all was that he hadn't had a college education. He almost cried when he said it.

He loved his family, yet he seemed to be constantly fighting with all of his three wives. When his third marriage was about to collapse, this very complex and emotional man would often vent violent anger toward his wife, then almost immediately turn around and pour his most tender love on his two young children. Tommy died suddenly in the midst of all this turmoil— he choked to death—a violent ending to a volatile life that, more than most people realized, contained many, many moments of sentimental caring.

I'm Gettin' Sentimental over You

Words by NED WASHINGTON
Music by GEORGE BASSMAN

I'm Glad There Is You

♩♩♩

Except for Sinatra, the most popular male vocalist with the big bands was Jimmy Dorsey's Bob Eberly. He had a wonderfully rich voice and a romantic way of phrasing, and, according to Frank himself, one of the reasons he decided as suddenly as he did to leave Tommy Dorsey and start his own career was to make the move before Eberly would.

Actually, Sinatra needn't have worried. Bob had neither the drive nor the ambition Frank had. As he once explained, "I was very content where I was, maybe in a lazy sort of way. But I never felt adequate, and perhaps it was that feeling that made me stay where I was. Anyway, I didn't want to leave. I was very happy making my four hundred dollars a week and twelve hundred and fifty dollars extra when we made movies."

One big reason for Eberly's happiness was his popularity—not only among his fans but even more so among his fellow-workers. He was probably the best-liked person ever to star on the big band scene—modest, unassuming, caring, with a wild sense of humor, especially about himself. And he loved Jimmy Dorsey and his musicians just as much as they loved him.

He had joined the band when it was still the Dorsey Brothers Orchestra and remained with it after Jimmy took over when Tommy walked off the bandstand and out of the band after one of the brothers' regular and often violent arguments. For several years, he was treated as just another vocalist, ambling over from his chair on the bandstand to the mike to sing one quick chorus in the middle of an arrangement. But as his popularity grew (he was constantly winning polls), Jimmy began to build entire arrangements around him, slowing down tempos so that he could phrase more effectively and utilizing the band more as a backdrop for Bob's performances.

A classic example of this treatment was the Dorsey band's "I'm Glad There Is You." As Eberly recently noted, "Many of the records that we made, we just sort of ground out. But there was a lot of time and heart put into this one.

"This was really a quality song. It had such a pretty lyric, kind of deep and poetic, maybe even a little too subtle for the times. And the melody itself was very good, too. I'd call it a high-I.Q.-style song."

Both the melody and lyrics were composed by Paul Madeira Mertz, who had played piano with the Dorseys and Bix Beiderbecke and all the other

"In this world of ordinary people,
extraordinary people. . . ."

stars in Jean Goldkette's famed band of the twenties. "I wrote the song over
a period of time," he recently revealed. "I had several different girls I was
going with in mind. [Alyce King of the King Sisters was one of them.] Eventually I decided to make a demonstration record of the tune and somehow
Jimmy heard it, liked it and said he wanted to record it. He had a manager
then, a very nice guy named Billy Burton, who thought it would help the
song if we listed Jimmy as one of the composers. He was probably right, but
Jimmy insisted that I receive one hundred percent of the royalties, and he
none—and that's how it's been to this day."

Dorsey's recording with Eberly's vocal turned out to be the most popular
version of the tune, though Alyce King's vocal with the Alvino Rey band
revealed a tremendous amount of emotion as well—and conceivably with
even greater justification. Throughout the years, "I'm Glad There Is You"
has remained a favorite among musicians and singers, as well as listeners
willing to let their hair down and admit to the sentiment that one extraordinary person can truly make life worth living.

I'm Glad There Is You

Words and Music by PAUL MADEIRA and
JIMMY DORSEY

I'm Gonna Sit Right Down
and Write Myself a Letter

♩♩♩

In addition to his talents as a songwriter (see comments on "Ain't Misbehavin' "), Fats Waller was a prodigious performer. An accomplished instrumentalist, whose stride piano style has been copied by many jazz musicians and admired by even more, he was also a wonderfully warm and witty entertainer.

One of Waller's greatest talents was his singing of pop tunes—not just those which he had written, like "Honeysuckle Rose," or those ideally suited to his humor, like his famed "Your Feet's Too Big"—but just about any song that happened to come along. He would poke fun at some syrupy ballad like "It's a Sin to Tell a Lie" and then turn right around and emote really touchingly on another sentimental tune like "I'll Never Smile Again," or swing like mad through "The Joint Is Jumpin'." But he was at his entertaining best when he blended his warmth and humor and, of course, his ever-swinging beat, as he did for one of his all-time hits, "I'm Gonna Sit Right Down and Write Myself a Letter," written by Joe Young and by one of the most prolific creators of hit tunes, the late Fred Ahlert, and, according to Fred Ahlert, Jr., a song that was "just lying on the shelf until Fats came along and turned it into a hit."

Fats worked closely with many of the musical greats, and they all loved him. He used to sit in with Louis Armstrong's band in its early days at the Grand Terrace Cafe in Chicago. He taught Count Basie how to play the organ in the old Lafayette Theater in Harlem. He wrote the music for Cab Calloway when he broke in at the Old Connie's Inn, also in Harlem. For a time he served as accompanist for the great Ethel Waters. He engaged in after-hours cutting sessions with the fabulous Art Tatum. He played the organ at the Cathedral of Notre Dame in France (he called it "the God Box"); exchanged courtesy calls and engaged in bull sessions with conductor Dimitri Mitropoulos; starred in the first big-time vaudeville show at New York's Academy of Music; hosted his own coast-to-coast radio series opposite Bing Crosby, with whom he also guested; toured all over England with the Mills Brothers; appeared in several movies, including *King of Burlesque* and *Stormy Weather;* and for ten years, starting in 1934, made hundreds of recordings for RCA Victor, most of them with a sextet, a few with a big band that he led for about a year.

". . . and make believe it came from you."

To the general public he may often have appeared as a buffoon, especially when he poked fun at or else ripped apart so many of Tin Pan Alley's triter tunes—which he did quite often and always justifiably. But to musicians who knew him and his music best, he was a pianistic giant. Perhaps nothing illustrates better the respect in which his peers held him than a remark attributed to Duke Ellington a long time ago when he was scheduled to perform on the same bill with Waller. "Please don't let him play," complained the great Ellington. "He'll show me up!"

But then, Fats was never *that* great—nobody was. Or, come to think of it, when you add up all his talents, including his prodigious piano technique, his spontaneous swing, his uninhibited exuberance, his infectious humor, and his savvy as a musician and entertainer, Duke might have had a little cause for a little worry at that!

I'm Gonna Sit Right Down and Write Myself a Letter

Words and Music by FRED E. AHLERT
and JOE YOUNG

Moderately *(with a lilt)*

I'm gon-na sit right down and write my-self a let-ter _____ And make be-lieve it came from you. _____ I'm gon-na

It Isn't Fair

♩♩♩

Most people associate "It Isn't Fair" with Sammy Kaye and Don Cornell. Actually the song had become quite popular before their 1950 recording, chiefly as the oft-heard theme song of an orchestra led by Richard Himber, who is listed as one of the tune's composers, and whose band, known as the Studebaker Champions, performed regularly for three years on the auto maker's commercial radio series.

"Cork" O'Keefe, one-time partner in the important Rockwell-O'Keefe booking office, can take indirect credit for the song's revival and prosperity. "After I sold out my interest in Rockwell-O'Keefe, I bought a music-publishing catalog called *Words and Music,* and one of its best songs was 'It Isn't Fair.' Naturally I wanted to have it recorded. Perry Como and I used to play golf regularly, and one day Sammy Kaye joined us. Perry was telling me he'd like to sing some of my songs on his radio show, especially 'It Isn't Fair,' and he said he'd even record it for me. Later, Sammy asked me, 'What was Como talking to you about?' And I told him.

"Well, several months later I was having a drink in the Gateway Restaurant in the RKO Building—you remember, that's where all the song publishers and artists used to hang out—and Herb Hendler, who was head of a. & r. for Victor, came over to me and said, 'Hey, you've got a big hit record.' I hadn't heard anything about it, so I asked him which of my songs, and he said, ' "It Isn't Fair," ' and I said, 'That Como, he's really something. He told me he'd record it, and now he's gone ahead and done it!' But Hendler said, 'No, Perry didn't record it; Sammy Kaye did.' " Apparently Kaye had been concentrating on more than just his putting that day on the course with Como and O'Keefe.

"What I remember most about the record," Kaye recently remarked, "was that it really made Don Cornell. He'd been with us since 1942—I first heard him with the McFarland Twins orchestra and I knew right then and there that I wanted him with my band—and so by the time 1950 had rolled around and he'd been with us for eight years, excluding time in military service, I knew it was time for him to go out on his own. 'You're beyond being just a band singer,' I kept telling him, and finally we decided he'd make just one more record date with our band and then he'd launch his own career."

Few singers ever had a better launching pad than the Kaye recording of

Sammy and·Don.

"It Isn't Fair." Not only did it do wonders for Don, but it also strengthened Sammy's own long and consistently successful career, which had begun in the early thirties with his own band at Ohio University and was to last for more than two generations.

It Isn't Fair

Words by RICHARD HIMBER
Music by RICHARD HIMBER, FRANK WARSHAUER
and SYLVESTER SPRIGATO

It's a Wonderful World

♩♩♩

One of the happiest-sounding songs of the big band era was "It's a Wonderful World," and one of the most joyous-sounding and also one of the best voices of the times was George Tunnell's. And who was George Tunnell? He was Bon Bon, the vital, cheery-voiced vocalist who sang "It's a Wonderful World" and many other songs with Jan Savitt's band, and who in the seventies was still singing in Philadelphia nightclubs for his appreciative hometown fans.

Savitt, a fine musician with a colorful background, was the son of a drummer in the Russian Imperial Regimental Band of the Czar, a child prodigy on the violin at the age of six, a top student at the famed Curtis Institute in Philadelphia, the youngest musician ever to play in the Philadelphia Symphony, and concert master under Leopold Stokowski.

In the mid-thirties, he switched from classical music to heading a big band, called the Top Hatters, which broadcast regularly from the studios of Philadelphia radio station KYW. Its reception was so tremendous that Savitt emigrated from the City of Brotherly Love to other cities around the country.

The band possessed four memorable features: (1) its shuffle rhythm,

"It's a wonderful world. . . ."   ". . . loving wonderful you!"

which produced a pushing, pulsating, eight-to-the-bar, instead of the usual four-to-the-bar, feeling; (2) a wonderfully warm, musicianly girl singer named Carlotta Dale; (3) the ebullient and talented Bon Bon; and (4) Savitt himself, an enthusiastic, articulate and extremely effective front-man.

"It's a Wonderful World" was written by Johnny Watson, the band's chief arranger, who had joined it during its Philadelphia period, and Harold Adamson, a noted lyricist, who had attended Harvard, and who wrote many hit tunes, including another Savitt standard, "720 in the Books," that also typified the happy sounds the band spread wherever it appeared.

It's a Wonderful World

Lyric by HAROLD ADAMSON
Music by JAN SAVITT and JOHNNY WATSON

It's Been a Long, Long Time

"Harry only had to hear that sixteen-bar theme once and he was sold," is how composer Jule Styne described Harry James's initial reaction to "It's Been a Long, Long Time." He was right. Harry was sold, so sold, in fact, that he recorded the tune almost immediately, Columbia released it almost immediately, and almost immediately it became a smash hit.

Why the big rush? Because World War II was ending, and servicemen were returning to their girls from all over the world. And every one of them could identify with those opening lines, "Kiss me once, and kiss me twice, then kiss me once again; it's been a long, long time."

James sure made the most out of the tune. He schmaltzed it up with his horn dripping musical chicken fat in front of a huge bank of sentimental-

Harry and Kitty.

sounding strings. And he let Kitty Kallen, his pretty new singer, wail her cute little heart out, openly inviting every serviceman to come back and reclaim what he'd been missing all those years.

By mid-1945, the James band had settled into a comfortable groove. For a time in mid-1943, right after Harry had married Betty Grable, it looked as if he might be drafted. But he was classified 4-F. Then six months later he was called back again for another examination. He was so sure he would be accepted that he put his entire band on notice. But at the last minute an old back injury disqualified him, and so he regrouped his forces. Since wars serve as superb breeding grounds for sentimentality, Harry began to concentrate more and more on ballads, much to the dismay of jazz lovers who wanted to hear more of his swinging trumpet.

After the war was over, however, and sentiment and longing were giving way to hope and joy, Harry began to return to his more swinging big band ways, and jazz lovers heaved sighs of relief as they seemed to agree that for James and jazz "It's Been a Long, Long Time."

It's Been a Long, Long Time

Lyric by SAMMY CAHN
Music by JULE STYNE

I've Heard That Song Before

Harry James had a tremendous instinct for always beating off the right tempo. Not everyone may always have agreed with him how fast or slow a song should go—certainly the composers of "I've Heard That Song Before" didn't—but Harry's sense of time invariably turned out to be correct. Perhaps his early training and experience as a drummer had some bearing; or

"We've heard that song before!"

maybe it was just his deep devotion to a good swinging beat. In any case, few if any bands could be as danceable and as bearable as Harry's.

When Jule Styne and Sammy Cahn presented Harry with their first collaborative effort, they thought he would treat it exactly the way he had Styne's "I Don't Want to Walk Without You." But Harry had other ideas. To him the song just didn't lay right as a slow, schmaltzy ballad. "I guess I surprised them," Harry admitted later, "and maybe even upset them a little bit. But to me that song was just great at a medium tempo with a real strong beat behind it."

How right was Harry? Some months after the record had been released, Columbia announced that it had sold a million and a quarter copies, the most in the label's history. But to this day, Styne hasn't given up his tempo fight. "If he'd played it slower, it would have been an even bigger hit," he recently insisted.

According to Cahn, who had teamed with Styne in 1942 to form one of the most successful of all songwriting teams, the title came to him the minute that Styne played the melody, and so he started half-singing the words, "I've heard that song before," whereupon Styne bristled, as though Cahn had accused him of stealing somebody else's melody, and almost resigned from the team before it had composed its first tune.

In addition to reaffirming James's talent for tempos, the recording also proved that Helen Forrest could do a first-rate singing job at a swinging tempo. To Harry, she was always "a real pro. And she was such a wonderful person! You know," he philosophized, "anyone with talent is nice. You never have trouble with people with talent. It's like baseball: It's those .210 hitters who give you your problems." And, he might have added, who don't stick around in the major leagues very long. Proof? More than three decades later, both Harry and Helen, two great pros, were still playing in top clubs throughout the country, each batting at least .300.

I've Heard That Song Before

Words and Music by JULE STYNE and
SAMMY CAHN

Moderato *(sweetly)*

It seems____ to me I've heard that song be - fore;____ It's from an old fa - mil-iar score, ____ I know it well, that mel-o - dy,_____ It's fun - ny

Just a Gigolo

Some of the most refreshing of the big band leaders were those who didn't take themselves too seriously, who had a lot of fun with their music and their fans, but who still maintained a high level of musicianship.

Of those, one of the best was Louis Prima, a first-rate jazz trumpeter out of New Orleans, who obviously adored his civic brother, Louis Armstrong, whom he imitated both instrumentally and vocally in a light, impish manner.

One of Prima's primary charms was that "I'm-having-a-lot-of-fun-doing-this-crazy-stuff-but-maybe-underneath-it-all-you'll-take-my-music-a-little seriously" approach. He made it plain that he was kidding when he sang his light, swinging versions of ballads—some of them quite sentimental and even morbid—and yet when he was finished you had the feeling that maybe there was a bit of the "Laugh, clown, laugh" longing welling there beneath the musical facade.

Such certainly was the feeling he projected whenever he performed "Just a Gigolo." Until Prima got hold of it, the song had been treated quite seriously. Written in 1931, one of its earliest and most famous recordings had been by Jack Hylton's large British orchestra, a rendition with a wailful lament from his heart-smitten vocalist. Its melodramatic message was also emoted in vaudeville houses and on radio programs throughout the English-speaking world. And then the song languished.

But along in the forties came Louis and his new approach. His band laid down a swinging, shuffle beat for its leader to tell the world how it felt to be a kept man. The only thing was, he did it so delightfully that you couldn't possibly imagine that he meant it. And yet, when it was all over, you began to wonder: Did he or didn't he?

The Prima formula was always light and a lot of fun, whether it came out as a quasi-lament or as one of the numerous novelties he used to sing with his attractive girl singers, Lily Ann Carol and Keeley Smith. And, because Louis surrounded himself with good players, his presentations were always musical.

As for your own interpretation of "Just a Gigolo"—well, you've got to make up your mind whether you want to take it seriously or whether, like Louis Prima, you feel that being just a gigolo isn't really such a bad life after all.

[175]

"Everywhere I go, people know the part I'm playing."

Just a Gigolo

English Words by IRVING CAESAR
Music by LEONELLO CASUCCI

Laura

One of the most haunting of all popular melodies didn't haunt its lyricist very much the first time he heard it. "I'd gone to a preview of the movie *Laura,* but I guess I wasn't too impressed," Johnny Mercer recently recalled, "because a couple of weeks later when Abe Olman of Robbins Music called and asked me if I'd like to write a lyric for the background theme they played in the picture, I told him I really didn't remember much about it. So Abe sent over a lead sheet, and I played the theme on and off for two or three weeks because by those days' standards it was a rather odd song. Finally I got used to it and loved it and started to write some lyrics. Abe had already impressed me that the title had to be 'Laura,' because people who had seen the picture and heard the theme had begun asking for 'the music from *Laura.*'"

When Mercer had completed his lyrics, he called composer David Raksin and asked him to drop over. Johnny, Glenn Wallichs and Buddy DeSylva had just started Capitol Records then. "I remember all I had then was a small office with a piano. Anyway, I sang the song for Raksin, and he said he loved it, but he'd like to make just one change. He asked me to use the word 'footsteps.'" All the rest of the words are Mercer's.

Johnny may have been unimpressed at first by the melody, but surely the success of the song has made a deep impression on him. "So far as I know," he admits, "it has been recorded more than any other song I've ever written. There must be at least four hundred records on that song."

One of the best and one of Mercer's favorites was also one of the first. Woody Herman recorded it in 1945, soon after the song had been written, at a time when the Herman Herd was making a reputation as the wildest, highest-swinging band of the era. But Woody treated "Laura" with tender restraint. He featured his Johnny Hodges–like alto, and Bill Harris' soulful trombone, but most of all his own voice. Few ballad singers out of the big bands could sing with as much emotion as Woody, and for "Laura" he really poured it on. Never was any song-titled girl ever treated with more loving care.

On the other hand, the Herman Herd projected much more violent sounds via its instrumentals. Featuring swinging, sometimes screaming ar-

"Laura!"

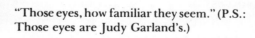

"A face in a misty light."

"Those eyes, how familiar they seem." (P.S.: Those eyes are Judy Garland's.)

rangements by Neal Hefti and Ralph Burns and others, it began to expand the borders of big band jazz, utilizing exciting, pulsating, modern harmonic and rhythmic concepts, as Woody, more than any of the other veterans of the swing era, kept insisting and proving that music need never stand still.

Laura

Lyric by JOHNNY MERCER
Music by DAVID RAKSIN

Let's Get Away from It All

♪♪♪

Few of the big bands ever had as much of a family feeling as did Tommy Dorsey's. And it was never more evident than on the band's recording of "Let's Get Away from It All."

This was the era when Tommy was fronting the best of all his bands, the one with Buddy Rich and Ziggy Elman and Joe Bushkin and the array of great singers: Frank Sinatra and Jo Stafford and the Pied Pipers and Connie Haines. A great spirit of camaraderie pervaded that 1941 edition of the Dorsey band, and though he wasn't actually in the band, a young songwriter and pianist named Matt Dennis was most welcome in its midst. On many a Sunday, Tommy would hold open house for his musicians, singers and business and personal friends at his Bernardsville, New Jersey, estate, not too far from Frank Dailey's Meadowbrook, where the band was playing. Invariably Matt would be there, too.

One thing about Tommy: When he became enthusiastic about something or someone, he'd go all out. Take electric trains, for instance. He was wild about them, and he'd buy paraphernalia by the cartons. Years later, while Tommy was showing me around his Connecticut home, we came across a slew of those cartons, stacked high in the rear of his garage. "Remember when I used to like electric trains so much?" he asked. "Well, those were some of the trains and tracks I never got around to unpacking."

For a time Matt Dennis was an equally important object of Tommy's enthusiasm. He had discovered this young songwriter, and he was going to let the whole world know about him. And so, in a period of ten days, Dorsey recorded four of Dennis' new songs: "Everything Happens to Me," featuring Sinatra; "Little Man with a Candy Cigar," featuring Jo Stafford; "Will You Still Be Mine," featuring Connie Haines; and a two-sided version of "Let's Get Away from It All," featuring *all* the singers—Frank, Jo, Connie and the Pied Pipers. Tommy's enthusiasm had really run rampant!

Fortunately for Matt, he fared much better than did Tommy's electric trains. Instead of going into storage, he soon began a career of his own, playing the country's top supper clubs and making several record albums. And he also continued to write more great songs, including "Violets for Your Furs," "Angel Eyes," and "The Night We Called It a Day," that stamped him as one of the era's more talented composers.

Tommy Dorsey has trouble getting away from *himself*!

Let's Get Away from It All

Lyric by TOM ADAIR
Music by MATT DENNIS

Make Believe Ballroom Time

♪♪♪♪

Glenn Miller always wanted to have a vocal group with his band. On one selection during its very first recording date in 1937—one that included a 24-year-old drummer named George T. Simon—Glenn used a vocal trio called the Tunesmiths. Later he tried forming a vocal quartet from within the band, including singers Tex Beneke, Gail Reese, and Ray Eberle and trombonist Paul Tanner, but it didn't work out. Still, Glenn kept hoping.

Enter Martin Block and his Make Believe Ballroom, a very popular and exceedingly influential disc jockey and his show on New York's famed radio station WNEW. Block, a seemingly self-assured and sometimes cocky-sounding personality, could and often did help to make lesser-known recording artists much better known simply by plugging their recordings. And one of those he supported, even before his group became the country's number one band, was Glenn Miller.

Still, Block, for all his influence, couldn't control everything. When ASCAP (the American Society of Composers, Authors and Publishers), in a fight over payments for use of its songs, withdrew permissions for radio stations to play them, Block had a problem. His theme song, *Make Believe Ballroom,* played by Charlie Barnet's Orchestra and sung by a then obscure vocal group called the Modernaires, became unavailable. What to do?

Songwriter Mickey Stoner, who had written a couple of tunes (*Faithful to You* and *I Guess I'll Have to Dream the Rest*) with Block listed as co-composer, had an obvious solution: "Let's write another theme song, one that won't be controlled by ASCAP." BMI (Broadcast Music, Inc.) had recently been formed as a clearing house to compete with ASCAP and was attracting writers and publishers.

Stoner and his partner, Harold Green, went to work and soon came up with *Make Believe Ballroom Time.* Block was impressed enough to call Miller to see if he wanted to record it. The leader, an astute businessman who obviously sensed Block's interest as well as his influence, replied "Sure," and suggested that they try to get the same vocal group that Barnet had used on *Make Believe Ballroom.*

Reenter Mickey Stoner. "The Modernaires had been singing with Paul Whiteman, but Whiteman wasn't working at the time. I found Chuck Goldstein [one of the group] in an advertising agency doing jingles. When I told him what we wanted, he immediately got the guys together and they had the song so well-

[190]

Glenn Miller (far left) in back of Make Believe Ballroom host Martin Block. Singers are (left to right) Hal Dickenson (hidden behind Bill Conway), Marion Hutton, Ralph Brewster, Tex Beneke and Chuck Goldstein. Bass player is "Doc" Goldberg.

rehearsed that when they went into the studio, they completed the recording in just one take!"

Obviously, Miller, a great appreciator of musical efficiency, was impressed. As Goldstein once reported, "By then Whiteman was about ready to give up his band, and when Glenn asked us if we'd like to join the band and go to Hollywood and make a movie, we asked Pops [Whiteman] to let us out of our contract. Well, you know what a sweetheart Whiteman was. Of course he let us go.

"The Mods consisted of one Presbyterian, Hal Dickenson; one Catholic, Bill Conway, who also played guitar; one Christian Scientist, Ralph Brewster, who played trumpet; and one Jew, me. We never read music. We heard everything in our heads. Bill would sit at the guitar or at the piano and we'd learn our songs that way. Hal Dickenson was the lead singer because he could only sing the melody. Sometimes I'd sing the harmony at the bottom, and sometimes I'd sing it way high up on top. Remember? Some people thought we had a girl with us."

Goldstein, the chubby, dark-haired lad who exuded an infectious joy, credits Glenn with giving the group a more commercial approach. "With Whiteman we always wanted to knock out musicians. Glenn kept saying, 'Always establish the melody. Then you can do your special material. But always come back to the melody.'" Miller's advice paid off. The Modernaires, after World War II and even with Glenn gone, became one of music's most successful vocal groups.

To this day, *Make Believe Ballroom Time,* by Miller and the Mods, remains that radio program's theme song.

Make Believe Ballroom Time

Lyric by MICKEY STONER
Music by HAROLD GREEN

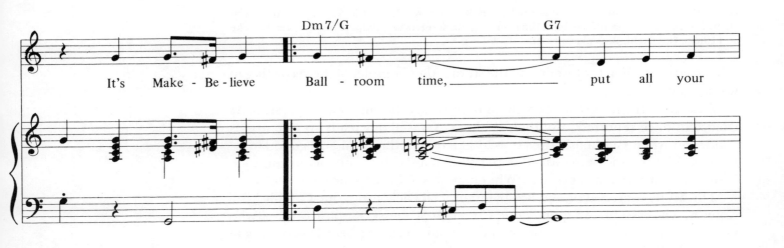

It's Make - Be - lieve Ball - room time, _____ put all your

cares a - way; _____ All the bands are here to

* Optional

Makin' Whoopee

♩♩♩

The most famous version of this delightfully witty warning was sung by Eddie Cantor, for whom the song was written by Gus Kahn and Walter Donaldson for a 1928 Broadway show called *Whoopee*. Cantor recorded it then, and he revived it two years later for the movie version of the musical comedy.

Though Cantor popularized the song, other name singers liked to do it—their way. According to Donald Kahn, the lyricist's son, "Dad was constantly writing new sets of lyrics for special artists. And people liked to make up their own lyrics as well." It seems everybody wanted to get into the makin' whoopee act.

During the big band days, however, the most fetching version was created by Tony Pastor, whose impish, little boy "no-I-really-didn't-steal-any-cookies" style of singing lent a delightful lilt to Artie Shaw's band, and then, after Artie had disbanded, became the focal point of Tony's own orchestra.

Born Antonio Pestritto, he had struck up a friendship with Shaw in their hometown of New Haven, Connecticut. "I was with a band led by John Cavallaro—Rudy Vallee played sax in the band also—and Artie, who was just a kid then, used to hang around, and he'd even carry my horn down to the railroad station for me."

When Shaw formed his first band in 1936, he asked Tony to play tenor sax and also to sing. One of the band's first record hits was an up-tempoed version of "Indian Love Call." Its feature: a vocal by Tony Pastor.

After Artie flew off to Mexico in 1939, leaving his band stranded, Pastor formed his own group. It was very musical, with good arrangements, musicians and singers, but for the general public its chief attraction remained Tony's impish, infectious, pixieish personality, which permeated such songs as "Let's Do It," "I'm Confessin'," " 'A,' You're Adorable," "Paradiddle Joe" and "Makin' Whoopee." In 1947 the band's vocal department was augmented by two cute girls from Cincinnati, Rosemary and Betty Clooney, with the former always crediting Tony's kindness and training as contributing to her eventual success as a recording star.

Pastor kept his band together longer than most of the big band leaders could. He featured his brother, Sal, on trumpet for a while, then finally

"Another season . . ."

". . . another reason . . ."

". . . for makin' whoopee!"

formed a smaller group that spotted two young, talented singers, Tony's sons, Guy and Tony, Jr. In between, of course, Tony, Sr., would continue to charm everyone with his delightfully impish manner until in 1969 a lingering illness stilled his voice forever.

Makin' Whoopee

Lyrics by GUS KAHN
Music by WALTER DONALDSON

Maybe

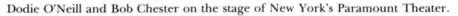

The Ink Spots had a big hit record of it. Sammy Kaye also recorded it. It was one of Dinah Shore's earliest and most impressive recordings. But the version of "Maybe," that timeless-sounding song of the mid-thirties, which impressed many big band followers most of all was the one by Bob Chester's band that featured a vocal chorus by Dolores O'Neill.

"Dodie," as she was called by her family and friends, even today enjoys a cult of dedicated fans. She was one of the most ethereal-sounding of all girl singers, and yet, despite that "little-dewey-eyed-girl-who's-just-come-in-out-

Dodie O'Neill and Bob Chester on the stage of New York's Paramount Theater.

of-the-mist" appeal, she also had a delightfully light, swinging beat. It was all there on Chester's recording of the very popular and especially singable "Maybe" as well as on dozens of other sides that Dodie made with the band.

Chester himself was a delightful man, though some of Glenn Miller's fans, and perhaps even Glenn as well, resented his unabashed aping of the Miller clarinet-lead sound. He had been a friend of many musicians for years, especially of Tommy Dorsey, and he had one advantage that few other bandleaders, except Charlie Barnet, had: He came from a very wealthy family and money was never a major worry for him.

His band never reached any great heights of popularity, though it was always musical and featured some good singers, including Dick Haymes' younger brother, Bob, and his brother-in-law-to-be, young Peter Marshall, a generation later the host of TV's "Hollywood Squares" game show. But for those who remember best, the voice in Bob Chester's band that they can never forget is that of Dodie O'Neill, and the way she sang "Maybe," and several dozen more songs of the era.

Maybe

Words and Music by ALLAN FLYNN and
FRANK MADDEN

Slowly *(with feeling)*

May - be you'll think of me, When you are all a - lone,_____ May - be the one who is wait - ing for you____ will prove un - true____ Then

Memories of You

♪♪♪

Songs with big intervals and big ranges often are avoided by singers who either don't have adequate vocal equipment or don't feel like taking unnecessary chances. On the other hand, musicians, especially those who enjoy displaying their virtuosity, are apt to latch on to such songs.

"Memories of You" is just such a song. It was first performed by a singer with great control and range, Ethel Waters, in a short-lived Broadway musical called *Blackbirds of 1930*. The melody was written by Eubie Blake, that master composer, pianist and charmer, who was playing piano and organ for rent parties at the turn of the century and seventy-five years later, at the age of ninety-two, still performing with equal charm and talent in public and on records. The lyrics came from Andy Razaf, also associated with Fats Waller, who reportedly had a thing going for one of the show's leading ladies, Minto Cato, who must have become the object of his affection, lyrics and memories.

Miss Waters recorded the song in 1930, and so did the great Louis Armstrong. But for many big band followers the most-heard and thus best-remembered version was blown by Sonny Dunham, the high-note trumpeter with Glen Gray and the Casa Loma Orchestra. This was a band that actually preceded Goodman, Dorsey and Shaw and all the rest in the hearts of the college kids, the first to very pointedly create mood changes by mixing exciting, if not always the greatest, up-tempoed jazz with warm, romantic ballads that featured soft clarinets, muted brass, an exceptionally pretty trombonist named Billy Rauch, and a handsome baritone vocalist named Kenny Sargent. In addition, it spotted several good jazz soloists: Dunham, clarinetist Clarence Hutchenrider, trumpeter Grady Watts, and trombonist Pee Wee Hunt, who later led his own successful dixieland group.

The band abounded in elegance. It often performed wearing tails, and after Gray emerged from the sax section to act as maestro, it sported one of the most handsome and personable of all bandleaders. Even before the start of the big band era—during 1933 and 1934—it was playing swing for the kids who packed the Glen Island Casino and for listeners of the Camel Caravan radio series.

The personnel of the band remained intact for years. One of the first to leave was Dunham, who for seven years had been featured on high-note trumpet numbers like "Memories of You," which he adopted as his new

Glen Gray and the Casa Loma band at the Glen Island Casino. Trumpeter at far left is Sonny
Dunham; trombonist at left is Peewee Hunt. Kenny Sargent is saxist at far right. Gray
(with mustache) sits in sax section as Mel Jensen conducts.

band's theme song. Sonny—his real name was Elmer—was an extremely intelligent, artistic, and intellectual man, whose suave personality didn't match
the fire of his playing. His band, though successful for a while, seldom projected the fire of Dunham's playing and eventually Sonny retired to a quiet
life in Florida.

The Casa Loma band also began to fade in the late forties, though Gray,
before he died in 1963, produced an impressive series of recordings for Capitol Records that successfully re-created the music of his orchestra and of
many of the swing era's other top bands.

Memories of You

Words by ANDY RAZAF
Music by EUBIE BLAKE

Minnie the Moocher

"We needed our own theme song for all those radio broadcasts we were doing from the Cotton Club, so Irving Mills and I sat down and wrote 'Minnie the Moocher.'"

Such is Cab Calloway's simple explanation of the origin of his biggest hit. "Originally, we had been using 'St. James Infirmary' as our theme, but we wanted something that was strictly our own. 'Minnie,' I want to point out, was a completely fictitious character, not a woman in my life, as some people seemed to think. Actually, the idea came from another song called 'Willie the Weeper' that had come out a few years before but had never become very popular."

Besides wailing effectively through blues-tinged epics like "Minnie the Moocher" and "St. James Infirmary," Calloway was a very emotional ballad singer. He also led a consistently fine band, whose alumni included Dizzy Gillespie, Jonah Jones, Ben Webster, Chu Berry and Cozy Cole. A well-educated man who had attended law school for a while, he used his rhythmic dancing style with his swinging hips, and his equally uninhibited shouting, to captivate the white audiences of the early thirties that would travel up to Harlem's Cotton Club. Later he went into the movies and nightclubs and the legitimate theater, highlighted by a magnificent portrayal of the character Sportin' Life in George Gershwin's classic *Porgy and Bess*.

But for the general public his "hi-de-ho" remained his identifying sound. "It was," he recently explained, "one of those damn things that just came up. I was always terrible at remembering lyrics, and sometimes I'd just throw in sounds like 'hi-de-ho.' Then, when I saw how people reacted, I decided to make it part of 'Minnie the Moocher.'"

"Minnie's been pretty good to me. She's about forty-five years old now and still going strong." Asked if she weren't about due for a change of life, Calloway retorted, "Her life has gone right along with mine, and I ain't changed nothin', man!"

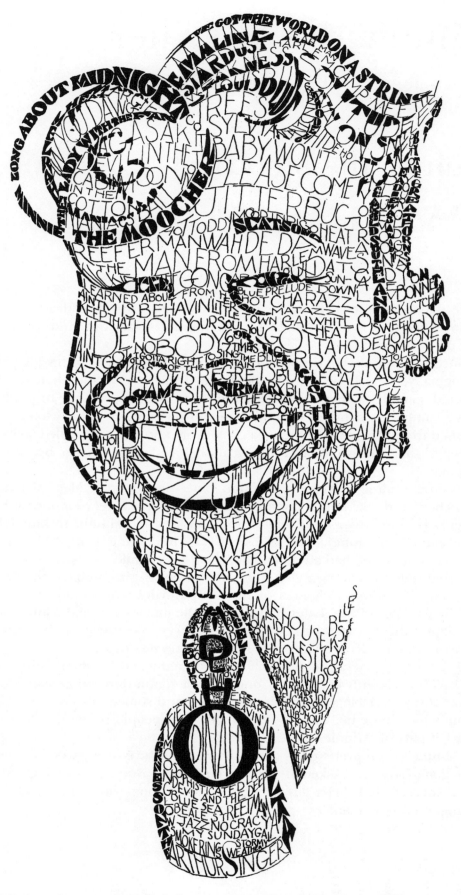

Cab Calloway's face promotes titles of tunes published by co-writer Irving Mills.

Minnie the Moocher

Words and Music by CAB CALLOWAY, IRVING MILLS
and CLARENCE GASKILL

Chorus

Mississippi Mud

♪♪♪

"Harry Barris wrote that tune," Bing Crosby recalled over the telephone from his California home. "He and Jimmy Cavanaugh. Harry was one of the Rhythm Boys, you know. Al Rinker and I had been singing with Paul Whiteman for, oh, I'd say, a couple of years, and then one night Whiteman heard Harry in the Olsen Club—that was run by George Olsen, the band-leader—in New York. Barris was doing a single, singing and slamming the piano and generally breaking things up. Whiteman thought he'd be good for the band, and so he teamed him up with Al and me and we became the Rhythm Boys."

The Rhythm Boys, the best and swingingest vocal group of the late twenties, were featured on numerous Whiteman recordings, but the one for which the trio is best remembered is its snappily arranged and performed version of "Mississippi Mud." "It became so associated with us," Bing pointed out, "that after we left Whiteman and went into vaudeville on our own, we used it sort of as a theme. We had this blown-up figure of Whiteman—it must have been at least seven feet high—and the lips moved as we were being introduced." Bing laughed as he recalled his early career in vaudeville. "You know, we were supposed to be a singing act, but in those days there were so many comedians on the bills that we developed into a talking act." But the theater managers didn't appreciate the Rhythm Boys' attempts at competitive humor, and so they soon went back to singing.

Whiteman, who had a fabulous ear for talent, discovered Crosby and Rinker in 1926 while they were working as a vocal duo in a competing Los Angeles theater. As a duo they were quite adequate. But Whiteman soon realized that Bing's baritone style (tenors were the rage in the popular music of the twenties) was not merely unique, but also musically intriguing. And so, even after the formation of the Rhythm Boys, he continued to feature him as a soloist, building him into such an attraction that by 1930 Bing was able to leave the band and soon thereafter to start his own fabulously successful career.

The Whiteman band developed many top stars, not merely because Pops, as he was affectionately known by those close to him, could recognize and appreciate talent, but also because, unlike other bandleaders, he promoted his singers and musicians. Thus, in addition to Crosby, he helped launch the

The beloved Pops.

The Original Rhythm Boys: Harry Barris, Bing Crosby, Al Rinker.

careers of singers Mildred Bailey, Morton Downey and Johnny Mercer, and instrumentalists Jimmy and Tommy Dorsey, Jack and Charlie Teagarden, Bix Beiderbecke, Joe Venuti and Eddie Lang, Henry Busse and others.

Obviously, Whiteman was also quite an innovator, and a gutsy one at that. He would try anything he believed in. His was the first dance band to popularize arrangements, to use full reed and brass sections, to play in vaudeville, to feature a girl singer and a vocal trio. Though older than most of the musicians with whom he associated (his professional playing career began all the way back in 1906), he was always anxious to keep up with the times, and eager to project into the future. At his fiftieth-anniversary recording date, when he was nearing seventy, and when veterans like the Dorseys and the Teagardens and Mercer and Venuti and others happily reassembled to honor their "Pops" and to record with him once more, Whiteman was still looking ahead. "As much as I enjoyed the past and appreciate the present," he said then, "it's the future that seems most important of all to me, because it's in the future that we ought to be able to create even greater music as we reap the benefits of our numerous mistakes and, I hope, of our even more numerous achievements."

Obviously, Paul Whiteman was one man whose feet would never be stuck in the Mississippi, or any other, mud!

Mississippi Mud

Words and Music by JAMES CAVANAUGH
and HARRY BARRIS

Interlude

Mood Indigo

♪♪♪

Those of us who were privileged to have known the great Duke Ellington found in him one of the freest of all spirits. He was a man who did things in his own way and his own time, whether it was composing, arranging, playing the piano, running an orchestra or just about anything else in his full and rich life. And, of course, whatever he did, he did magnificently and elegantly and strictly in the Duke Ellington manner. Never in the history of the big bands was there a more powerful, all-encompassing, influential musical creator, and it is doubtful if the likes of him will ever exist again.

One never knew what to expect from Duke, and least of all *when* to expect it. He was notorious—and self-admittedly so—as a last-minute provider, whether it was an extended suite for an important concert, an appearance for a radio or television show, an involved arrangement for a recording date or just one of the dozens upon dozens of magnificent songs that he composed.

The most famous of Duke's early compositions was "Mood Indigo," which like many others written by Ellington, was completed just before a recording date, this one on the afternoon of October 30, 1930. As Duke relates it in his autobiography, *Music Is My Mistress:*

> On this occasion, as usual, the night before was the time for me to write and think music. I already had three tunes and, while waiting for my mother to finish cooking dinner, I began to write a fourth. In fifteen minutes, I wrote the score for "Mood Indigo." We recorded it, and that night at the Cotton Club, when it was almost time for our broadcast, Ted Husing, the announcer, asked, "Duke, what are we going to play tonight." I told him about the new number, and we played it on the air, six pieces out of the eleven-piece band. The next day, wads of mail came in raving about the new tune, so Irving Mills put a lyric on it, and royalties are still coming in for my evening's work more than forty years later.

Though always closely associated with the Ellington sound—in this case the tightly muted trumpet and trombone along with the subtone clarinet, all cooing gently around a microphone—"Mood Indigo" has also surfaced as a complete song for sensitive singers searching for something special. One of its most memorable versions was recorded some years ago by Frank Sinatra, in which he began with the chorus, then went into the verse and finally returned to the chorus—a routine strongly recommended to those of you who also wish to participate in this Ellington masterpiece.

The Duke.

Mood Indigo

Words and Music by DUKE ELLINGTON,
IRVING MILLS and ALBANY BIGARD

Moonglow

♩♩♩

"It happened very simply," Will Hudson explained from his home in Florida, where he's now living comfortably on his royalties and ASCAP checks. "Back in the early thirties, I had a band at the Graystone Ballroom in Detroit, and I needed a theme song. So I wrote 'Moonglow.'"

Hudson's band was no huge success, so he migrated to New York and

Will to Eddie: "Can't you ever make it on time?"

began writing and arranging for Mills Music. "Mostly I'd do scores and some originals for Jimmie Lunceford, Cab Calloway, Fletcher Henderson, Benny Goodman and other leaders." But all this time he hadn't forgotten about his own band's theme, and one day Mills suggested that a young lyricist, a recent Phi Beta Kappa graduate from the University of Pennsylvania, put some words to the tune. "That's how Eddie DeLange and I first got together," Will recalls. "At the time, Eddie was leading a small band out at Rockaway Beach. The next summer he got a job at Roadside Rest out on Long Island. But most of the time all his band did was fake or jam. So at the end of the season, the owner told him either improve his music or else. . . ."

The "or else" being entirely unacceptable to DeLange, he decided to use arrangements in his band. So he turned to his collaborator and asked Will if he'd like to take over the band's musical direction. And that's how the Hudson-DeLange partnership-band was formed. Its new relaxed, self-composed swinging style created quite a furor at Roadside Rest, and by 1936 the band had been blessed with a slew of coast-to-coast radio broadcasts and a Brunswick recording contract.

For their theme song the partners used one of Will's instrumental originals called "Sophisticated Swing," whose light, gentle lilt typified the band's approach to swing. For its ballads, it turned to airy clarinets, often blown in unison, muted brass, and some good singers, like Ruthie Gaylor, Nan Wynn, and Fredda Gibson, who later changed her name to Georgia Gibbs and became a radio and recording star on her own. DeLange, a colorful leader (he had red hair, a red mustache and a wild, joyous grin), also sang some of the ballads in a pleasant, whisky-type way.

Though they collaborated well musically, Hudson and DeLange had trouble getting along together personally. Will was reserved and conservative; Eddie flamboyant and swinging in many more ways than in his music. "I guess maybe it was a mistake to split up then, but I just couldn't take it any longer," Will recently confessed.

Each formed his own band; neither succeeded. They tried getting together again in 1941, but nothing happened, and even before the big band era ended a few years later, the Hudson-DeLange band had become nothing but a very pleasant memory.

However, not so "Moonglow." In 1956, Steve Allen, in writing the theme song for the movie *Picnic,* composed a counter-melody to "Moonglow," and often thereafter the Hudson-DeLange "oldie" and the Allen "newie" could be heard simultaneously on records, radio, television and juke boxes.

Moonglow

Words and Music by WILL HUDSON, EDDIE
DE LANGE and IRVING MILLS

Moonlight Serenade

♩♩♩

When Glenn Miller wrote "Moonlight Serenade," he had no idea his melody would ever have such lyrics, or any lyrics at all, for that matter, or that it would become one of the most evocative theme songs of the big band era. For Glenn, then studying arranging with Joseph Schillinger, had written the tune as a mathematical exercise in composition—the Schillinger system revolved around such a nonromantic approach—and he had nothing more in mind than to complete a specific portion of the course he was taking. And at that time, 1935, he didn't even have a band!

But the exercise must have pleased him, because he sought out Eddie Heyman, who had written the words to "Body and Soul," and asked him to write a set for his new melody. Eddie obliged with some very pretty though sad lyrics, and for a while the song was known as "Now I Lay Me Down to Weep."

Glenn had joined Ray Noble's band by this time. Its singer was a very sentimental crooner named Al Bowlly, one of the finest balladeers of the era, and I can still remember the night Bowlly cornered me in the Noble band's dressing room and sang, unaccompanied, except for a few tears in his eyes, Miller's "new song."

Glenn made a few halfhearted attempts to get his new tune played. He took it to his old cronies, the members of the Bob Crosby band with whom he had played when they were all part of Ben Pollack's orchestra, but they told him that his arrangement didn't fit their instrumentation, and after that Glenn pretty much forgot about his Schillinger exercise.

Then in 1937 he formed his own orchestra, and, of course, he needed a theme song. That's when he forgot about forgetting about his song. But "Now I Lay Me Down to Weep" was too melancholy a thought for a theme song, he figured, so he set about looking for other lyrics.

One set, called "Gone with the Dawn," written by the guy who's sitting here writing this story right now, also proved to be too depressing. In the meantime, Glenn had assigned the tune to Robbins Music, who in turn asked Mitchell Parish, the lyricist of "Star Dust" and so many other hits, to provide the words. Parish came up with a set called "Wind in the Trees," and those might have been the permanent lyrics except that Abe Olman, Robbins' professional manager, had a sudden brainstorm: Glenn was about to record

The Moonlight Serenader.

Frankie Carle's "Sunrise Serenade." "Why not back it with something appropriate, like 'Moonlight Serenade'?" Again Parish was called in, and again he delivered.

Glenn's recording was strictly instrumental, focusing on the lovely clarinet-led reed section. Except for a period when songs licensed by ASCAP were forbidden to be aired on the networks and Glenn substituted the non-ASCAP "Slumber Song," all of his broadcasts began with this lovely melody, one that probably has raised more goose pimples for more people who participated in the big band era than any other song ever written.

Moonlight Serenade

Lyric by MITCHELL PARISH
Music by GLENN MILLER

Nighty-Night

♩ ♩ ♩

One of the coziest send-offs at the end of any late-night big band remote broadcast was this pretty ballad, cooed softly by Yvonne King and the rest of the King Sisters when they were members of the Alvino Rey band of the early forties. Written by the veteran Joe Davis, it served as the closing theme for one of the most tightly knit groups of musicians and singers.

Some of them—Alvino, arranger-saxist Frank DeVol, guitarist Dick Morgan and the four Kings—had worked with Horace Heidt and His Musical Knights, where they had struck up unusually warm friendships. Alvino soon married Louise King, and after Heidt fired Alyce King because, according to Rey, "she accidentally knocked over a mike and it hit a girl who was dancing by," several members of the warm friendship group exited also, later to re-form under Rey.

Alvino's real name was Al McBurney. He wasn't Latin at all ("I hate Latin music!" he once exclaimed), but half-Scotch and half-Irish, with a wild sense of humor. His band reflected his personality. There was a great deal of

The King Sisters—Alyce, Louise, Donna and Yvonne—and Alvino.

joshing going on, but though the atmosphere was always relaxed and homey, the music never suffered. The group's brain trust of Rey, an excellent guitarist who used electronics uniquely and effectively, DeVol, who later became one of Hollywood's foremost arrangers, Morgan, saxist Skeets Herfurt and pianist Buddy Cole (he later married Yvonne King) consisted of dedicated, imaginative, highly responsible musicians, so that the quality of the band's music and entertainment remained high. Successive reviews in *Metronome* magazine tabbed it (1941) "The No. 1 'Never-a-Dull-Moment' Aggregation of Dancebandom" and (1942) "The finest of all Show Bands."

During the war, Alvino and many of his fellow bandsmen got jobs together in an aircraft factory. When not working on spare parts, they devoted their spare time not only to keeping up the band but also to enlarging it. Rey recalls, "We must have wanted to out-do Stan Kenton. We had six saxes and ten brass and seven vocalists. Billy May, Nelson Riddle and George Handy wrote our arrangements."

But the American Federation of Musicians' recording ban was then in effect, so the band couldn't record, and, with such a large payroll, it soon was forced to disband. Later Alvino and the King Sisters appeared for many seasons on television as members of the King Family series, which included not only their children but also their children's children.

And how did each program end? With Yvonne leading them all through "Nighty-Night," of course.

Nighty-Night

Words and Music by
JOE DAVIS

Oh Johnny, Oh Johnny, Oh!

♪ ♪ ♪

By inserting a few extra panting "oh's" and a few insinuating "uh-uh's" into a World War I hit, Wee Bonnie Baker succeeded in transforming previously G-rated "Oh Johnny, Oh Johnny, Oh!" into a PG-rated top-selling record of 1939.

Three years earlier, Orrin Tucker, who'd studied to be a doctor before he became a bandleader, had found Evelyn Nelson of Orange, Texas, singing in his hometown of St. Louis, Missouri, and asked her to join his band. He changed her name to Bonnie Baker, and for three years they both led pleasant if unexciting careers. And then it happened:

The band was playing in the swank Empire Room of Chicago's Palmer House, which featured, along with dancing, a nightly revue that included a line of chorus girls prancing prettily while Bonnie sang demurely in the background. But for some reason or other, on one special production number the customers began paying more attention to Bonnie's singing than to the dancers. So a few nights later, at the producer's insistence, up front and center pranced Bonnie singing "Oh Johnny, Oh Johnny, Oh!" And from then on, night after night, using the same coy, cute, cozy, cuddly approach and emphasizing those extra "oh's" and "uh-uh's," she captivated the patrons. Orrin, recognizing the power and appeal of well-orchestrated sighs and pants, immediately featured Bonnie and "Johnny" on his radio broadcasts and soon thereafter created the hit recording that eventually catapulted Tucker and his tiny, titillating, tantalizing thrush into the top stratosphere of the Hit Parade.

But that wasn't the first time "Oh Johnny" had swept the nation. Back in 1916, a young composer named Abe Olman had tried unsuccessfully to popularize the tune he and Ed Rose had written. He failed. Then a more experienced publisher, Fred Forster, latched on to it, and under his direction young Olman, turned song-plugger, succeeded in convincing top stars to sing his tune. Eddie Cantor sang it. Al Jolson sang it. Sophie Tucker sang it. Ted Lewis sang it. It was featured in George White's Scandals and in the Ziegfeld Follies. In that era, recordings were not the barometer of a song's popularity—sheet music sales were, and "Oh Johnny, Oh Johnny, Oh!" sold an almost unheard of million and a quarter copies!

In 1918, Olman, who later became one of the big band era's most success-

"Oh Bonnie, Oh Bonnie, how you can slice!"

ful music publishers, had become increasingly patriotic and also quite weary of constantly plugging and hearing his song. So he enlisted in the army. And what were the first sounds he heard upon arriving at training camp? A bunch of rookie soldiers marching to the tempo of—you guessed it—"Oh Johnny, Oh Johnny, Oh!"

Oh Johnny, Oh Johnny, Oh!

Words by ED ROSE
Music by ABE OLMAN

Moderately bright
Verse

All the girls are cra-zy 'bout a cer-tain lit-tle lad,____ Al-tho' he's ver-y, ver-y bad,____ He could be, oh so good when he want-ed to. Bad or good he un-der-stood 'bout love and oth-er things,____ For ev-'ry

On the Sunny Side of the Street

♪♪♪

"You know, one of the things I liked so much about working for Tommy Dorsey," Sy Oliver, one of the big bands' most creative and respected arrangers, was saying recently, "was the way he let you go ahead and do things on your own. You hear talk about how rough Tommy could be, but if you did your job right, there'd never be any trouble.

"Take 'On the Sunny Side of the Street,' for example. I'd always liked the tune and so I just decided to go ahead and write a new arrangement. I remember when I brought it into rehearsal. We were out in Chicago, and as I started to run through the number for the first time with the band—Tommy always let me rehearse my own things—Tommy was just about to leave. In fact, he was just going out the door when the horns hit that bright introduction with the sustained strings underneath, and Tommy turned right around and yelled, 'What was THAT!' And he came back and stayed for the entire rehearsal."

Certainly the 1944 Oliver treatment of the lovely ballad by Dorothy Fields and Jimmy McHugh, written for the 1930 Broadway show *The International Revue,* never had, and for that matter never has, received such a delightfully light, swinging treatment. That was part of the Oliver charm. He could take almost any tune, even an old war horse, like "Swanee River," for example, and imbue it with a rollicking, though never raucous beat. He had created this style while he was with the Jimmie Lunceford band, and was writing one successful arrangement after another. But after a while, Sy had grown tired of the road and was preparing to leave Lunceford and return to college when Dorsey invited him up to his hotel room. "I remember he was shaving, and he turned to me and said, 'Sy, whatever you are making with Jimmie, I'll pay you $5,000 a year more.' I said, 'Sold!' and that was it." Today, Sy is still trying to find time to go back to college.

Dorsey's admiration of Sy in general and of his arrangement of "On the Sunny Side of the Street" in particular was obvious. When the musician union's two-year recording ban was lifted in November 1944, the first number the Dorsey band recorded was this Oliver creation, featuring a swinging vocal interpretation by four sisters who called themselves The Sentimentalists. Some months later, one of them left to raise a family, and nobody has ever explained whether or not Sy had anything to do with hiring

Sy Oliver, far left, plus arranger-saxist Fred Stulce, Tommy, and arranger Axel Stordahl.

her replacement. In any case, Lillian Clark later became Mrs. Sy Oliver, and she turned out to be an important, supportive influence in the emergence in the early seventies of the Sy Oliver band, which continued to play its leader's infectiously swinging sounds to the delight of his old and new enthusiastic fans.

On the Sunny Side of the Street

Lyric by DOROTHY FIELDS
Music by JIMMY McHUGH

Racing with the Moon

♩♩♩

Few bands ever arrived on the big band scene with as much ballyhoo as Vaughn Monroe's. Prior to its big-time debut at Frank Dailey's Meadowbrook in the spring of 1941, it had been formed and carefully groomed in and around Boston, where Vaughn had been making a reputation as a singer and trumpeter. Then a carefully planned campaign introduced it to the rest of America.

The reaction was great—not so much for the band, which needed, and eventually showed much improvement, as for Vaughn himself. An extremely handsome, well-built man, with an ingratiating smile and touches of a little boy's shyness, he appealed to women of all ages. His voice, though seldom

"R-r-r-acing with the moon! . . ."

praised by critics, projected virility, vitality and even touches of tenderness, and it became the focal point of his band, his trumpeting soon relegated to just a few bars here and there.

The intense way he sang his theme, "Racing with the Moon," with its quasi-operatic overtones, typified his vocal style. The dramatics of the song, written especially for him by arranger Johnny Watson and Johnny's wife, Penelope Pope, made this an ideal vehicle.

Vaughn's singing style may have made him appear a bit pompous and stiff. But, according to sidemen Wedo Marasco and Joe Conni, who played with the band for many years, off the stand and away from any microphones he was a relaxed and very wonderful gentleman. Said Marasco, "No one wanted to leave the band, he treated us so well. We would travel by Pullman instead of coach, or we'd fly, and, unlike other bands, we didn't have to pay for any part of our uniforms. If a guy needed money, Vaughn would loan it to him with no interest. If anybody had a problem, even some of the band wives, Vaughn would say, 'What can I do to help?' And then he'd help as best he could."

Vaughn was also a smart man. Though he never lost his appreciation of good music, and, one suspected, still wanted to show the world that he could play good trumpet too, he saw to it that his performances focused more and more on singing.

Thus, when the big band sound gave way to the singers' sound in the latter forties, Vaughn, still concentrating more on vocal than instrumental chords, survived very comfortably and longer than some of the more famous, instrumentally oriented bandleaders.

Racing with the Moon

Words by VAUGHN MONROE and PAULINE POPE
Music by JOHNNY WATSON

Scatter-brain

♩♩♩

What began as a warmup exercise for a trombone player each evening before he started his job turned out to be one of the most popular songs of 1939.

Kahn Keene was the trombonist, and he was then a member of Frankie Masters' band. (Later he became one of the Crew Chiefs, the vocal group in Glenn Miller's AAF orchestra.) As Keene, now working with his own small group in Savannah, Georgia, recently said, "Carl Bean, who was arranging for the band, used to hear me do that warmup, and he said he liked it and suggested we write it out. We did, and I kept the manuscript in my briefcase.

"Sometime later we were playing in the Roosevelt Grill in New York, and Frankie was looking for material for the band's first record date. So I dug

Maestro Masters.

the tune out of my case and Carl made an arrangement of it, and we tried it out in the Grill. Chester Conn, a music publisher, heard the tune and liked it right away, and he got Johnny Burke, who had been writing all those great songs for Bing Crosby, to do some lyrics. He finished them one day and the next day we recorded the song.

"Now, here's something interesting. Johnny and I wrote this song together, but we never got to meet each other!" Burke's name, of course, appears on the sheet music. So does Bean's, who made the arrangement. And so does Masters'. "He just went along for the ride, I guess," remarked Keene. "A lot of bandleaders did that in those days."

Masters happened to be an exceptionally nice, pleasant gent. His was never an outstanding band, content more to play simple, straightforward dance music for simple, straightforward folks, rather than going in for any heavily stylized renditions. He had two good girl singers, first Marion Francis and then Phyllis Myles, whom he later married. But most of the vocal spotlight fell on Masters, who invariably delivered songs like "Scatter-brain" in a friendly, informal, "You-know-I-wouldn't-harm-a-flea" fashion. And he wouldn't.

Scatter-brain

Words by JOHNNY BURKE
Music by KAHN KEENE, CARL BEAN and
FRANKIE MASTERS

talk it's so in-sane,   Still it's charm-ing chat - ter, Scat - ter-
bout the third re-frain, Then you·start your pat - ter, Scat - ter-

brain.   I know I'll end up ap-o-plec-tic but there's
brain.   Per-haps I'm much too an-a-lyt-ic but I'm

noth-ing I can do, it's just the same as be-ing in a hur-ri-
up the well known tree; I've tried to un-der-stand your dou-ble talk in

Sent for You Yesterday

♪ ♪ ♪

According to one of its composers, one of the biggest blues hits of the big band era came out of a joke. "Somebody in the band was always coming in late, so Jimmy, who was always making up lyrics, came out with 'Sent for You Yesterday, Here You Come Today,'" revealed Eddie Durham, arranger, trombonist and part-time guitarist in that band. "Then later we made a song out of it, only this time instead of being for a musician, it was for some chick or other."

Durham, a brilliant arranger, who also worked for Jimmie Lunceford and Glenn Miller, was reminiscing about Count Basie's great 1938 band, and about the late Jimmy Rushing, the fabulous blues shouter, who sang "Sent for You Yesterday" on the Basie record—and probably close to 10,000 times thereafter.

He had been singing with Basie even before the band had emigrated from Kansas City in 1936 to astound the big band world with its supple, free-swinging jazz, and he stayed with it until 1948, when he left to start his own career. But his impact on the band lived on for years.

More than a generation later, in 1971, Basie was still reveling in the memory of his association with Rushing and the possibilities of occasional reunions at concerts. "He was the gem of the ocean. He could always swing the blues. Right now we look forward so much when we know we're going to work with him. The time can't go too fast, because we know we're going to have some fun."

Of course, for swing band lovers, the time can never go too fast to hear the entire Basie band. Since the mid-thirties, it has consistently produced the highest-swinging of big band sounds. When it first arrived in New York back in 1936, its musicianship may have distressed some critics, who faulted its out-of-tune playing. But even then, none could deny the band's tremendous rhythmic impact nor the exceptional jazz contributions of saxophonists Hershel Evans and Lester Young, trumpeter Buck Clayton, and of the loosest, swingingest rhythm section of the era, featuring Basie on piano, along with guitarist Freddy Green, bassist Walter Page and drummer Jo Jones.

Though it has played many original instrumentals by Neal Hefti, Quincy Jones and others written especially for the band, and though it has toured with and played backgrounds for Frank Sinatra and Tony Bennett and other

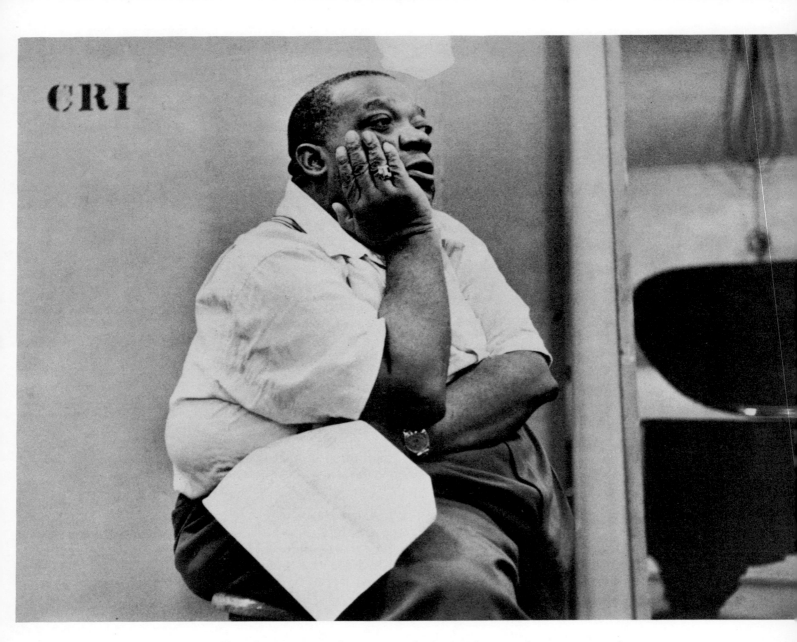

CRI

"Sent for You Yesterday" . . . and whatever happened to you, anyway?

top singers, and though it has also played its share of pop tunes, the Basie band's chief stock-in-trade has always been the twelve-bar blues—disguised sometimes by thematic variations, but crystal clear to musicians and all others who recognize those time-honored chord progressions that have been the basis for much of rock and almost all of rhythm-and-blues music.

Basie's emphasis on the blues isn't entirely emotional. He loves them, but he also recognizes them as a sure way of his band's never fading away. "There'll always be room for the blues," he recently pointed out. "Maybe there'll be some slight changes, like a little note here and a little note there, but it's still the blues and it still makes it and it always will. For there's one thing that will never die, and that's the blues!"

Sent for You Yesterday
(and Here You Come Today)

Words and Music by JIMMY RUSHING, COUNT
BASIE and ED DURHAM

Don't the moon look lone - some, shin -
- in' through the trees? Don't the moon look lone - some, shin -

Sentimental Journey

♪♪♪

"Sentimental Journey," one of the biggest hits of the war years, especially when pretty Doris Day cooed it in her soft, sexy way, might never have been written if Ben Homer hadn't needed some money.

Ben was Les Brown's arranger, and when Buddy Morris, a publisher friendly with many of the bands, heard that Homer needed cash, he said, "Why don't you write a song. I'll give you an advance, and you can use our office to work."

"I was living in the Whitby Apartments on West Forty-fifth Street then," remembers Les, who is still leading his band on occasion but more often living and playing golf and bridge with the entertainment elite of California. "And one day I got a call from Ben. He said he had an idea for a song and why didn't I come over and we could work on it." So over to the Morris office went Brown. "All Ben really had was a skeleton. But we did work on it together, and I remember I came up with that Sears Roebuck release—you know, very obvious and stereotyped and cliché-ridden—but I made one mistake: I made the song too rangy."

Doris Day, though, was even then an exceptionally good singer who wasn't easily discouraged. "Sentimental Journey," big range and all, really appealed to her, and she wasn't going to let a few extra high notes get in her way. But, the first time she and the band ran through the arrangement, the reaction was pretty nil. "It was at one of those late-night rehearsals. Nobody else seemed too impressed," Doris recalls. But when the band began playing the song for the dancers in the Cafe Rouge of the Hotel Pennsylvania, her and Les's faith was vindicated. The kids loved it. "I was pretty sure we had a hit on our hands," says Les. "But we couldn't play it on the air, either, because I didn't want some other band to get the tune and possibly record it before we could."

On the band's first session, following the lifting of the recording ban, it waxed "Sentimental Journey." Les and Doris again were absolutely correct. The orders poured into Columbia Records. According to Les, "They told us we could have sold three million copies, but those were the war years and they couldn't get enough shellac." Eventually, of course, the shellac shortage abated. But not the sales of the highly evocative "Sentimental Journey," the song that might never have been written if a certain young arranger just hadn't happened to run out of cash, and might never have become a hit if a certain young singer hadn't happened to sing it with so much feeling.

Les and Doris.

Sentimental Journey

Words and Music by BUD GREEN, LES BROWN
and BEN HOMER

Very slowly

Gon - na take a sen - ti - men-tal jour-ney, Gon - na set my
heart at ease,__ Gon - na make a sen - ti - men-tal jour-ney
To re-new old mem - o - ries.__ Got my bag, I

Serenade in Blue

♩♩♩

Mack Gordon and Harry Warren wrote "Serenade in Blue" for the Glenn
Miller band in its second movie, *Orchestra Wives,* another example of a tune
being well tailored, as Warren liked to put it, for the particular occasion. For
few songs in the large Miller repertoire ever provided such a stellar setting
for the gorgeous Miller clarinet-led reeds as this number. The movie rendition also included singing by Ray Eberle and Pat Friday (dubbing for actress
Lynn Bari) and the commercial recording spotted Eberle minus Friday, but

Glenn and Ray.

it was those soaring reeds at the start of the opening chorus that invariably evoked (they still do, for that matter) spontaneous cheering.

That lead-clarinet-over-four-saxophones musical formula prevails, even two generations after its discovery, as the dance band era's most distinctive musical voicing. In *The Glenn Miller Story,* the movie of Glenn's life, Hollywood presented the birth of that sound at a Miller band rehearsal. Actually, Glenn discovered it before he even had a band, while he was still arranging for Ray Noble's band. During an exclusive interview in 1939, soon after that sound had begun to entrance listeners everywhere, Glenn divulged its origin. "Peewee Erwin, now playing trumpet for Tommy Dorsey, was with us in the Noble band. At the time, Peewee had a mania for playing high parts; he always asked me to give him stuff written way up on his horn. Sometimes I'd write things [i.e., the melody lead] for him with the saxes playing underneath.

"There came a day when Peewee left and a trumpeter who couldn't hit those high notes replaced him. In desperation, we assigned those B-flat trumpet parts to Johnny Mince, now also with Tommy Dorsey, on B-flat clarinet and doubled the clarinet lead with Danny D'Andrea [a violinist who doubled on reeds] an octave lower on tenor sax. That's how the clarinet-lead sound, which people call 'our style,' started."

The Noble band seldom utilized that voicing. But when Glenn, in 1938, after having failed with his first band, began looking for a distinctive, identifiable sound he recalled the Noble experiment. So he began to build all his ballads' arrangements around this voicing, and by the spring of 1939 the public responded precisely as Glenn hoped it would. One big hit soon began to follow another, though none of them utilized that lead-clarinet style any more effectively than the gorgeous Miller version of "Serenade in Blue."

Serenade in Blue

Words by MACK GORDON
Music by HARRY WARREN

Somebody Else Is Taking My Place

♪♪♪

Russ Morgan was a first-rate musician. He played piano, trombone, vibes, organ, sax and guitar. He was a conductor and an arranger. He played trombone in the Detroit Symphony, and he also played trombone in, and wrote arrangements for, the famous Jean Goldkette band that included Bix Beiderbecke and other top jazz stars of the late twenties. He was the musical director for a radio station and then for a top recording company, and he conducted for several radio series, including the Phillip Morris program. He also led his own band in some of the country's top hotel rooms and broadcast regularly, beginning each show with the same pronouncement: "It's Music in the Morgan Manner!" after which he would gliss languidly on his trombone, adding a few identifying wah-wahs, and the show would go on.

Morgan was also a talented songwriter, who combined his musical knowledge with a fine commercial sense. He wrote, among many songs, his theme, "Does Your Heart Beat for Me," "You're Nobody Till Somebody Loves You," "So Tired" and his biggest success, "Somebody Else Is Taking My Place," which was also recorded by two of his good friends, Benny Goodman, with a fine vocal by a young Peggy Lee, and Claude Thornhill, with some wildly humorous piano-playing by Claude. Goodman and Thornhill and Morgan had all worked together in New York's radio and recording studios,

"Wah-wah" Morgan.

along with Tommy and Jimmy Dorsey, Artie Shaw and Bunny Berigan—before any of them had formed their big bands.

Russ started his band after a stay with Freddy Martin's, primarily to exploit the wah-wah style of tromboning he had begun to perfect, and conceivably because it would give him a chance to sing in his distinctive, ingratiating, rasping manner, without possible interference from a leader who might not appreciate such self-indulgence. For Morgan was never beyond enjoying himself, even if it might mean sacrificing some of his musical standards. Thus, his band, though somewhat commercially successful, never reflected the high caliber of musicianship which he was capable of projecting. But then, who could really blame Russ, who had finally emerged from early poverty among the coal mines of his native Pennsylvania to find a brighter life, and personal and financial recognition in the world above ground.

Somebody Else Is Taking My Place

Words and Music by DICK HOWARD, BOB
ELLSWORTH and RUSS MORGAN

Star Dust

Probably the most popular song of all time wasn't a complete song for several years. Hoagy Carmichael had written "Star Dust" as an instrumental composition in the mid-twenties back home in Indiana. "I had no idea what star dust meant," he later admitted, "but I thought it would make a gorgeous title."

He recorded the tune—without words, of course—as pianist in Emil Seidel's Orchestra for the defunct Gennett label. Hoagy was a jazz buff, and his instrumental was then performed at an up tempo, with none of the romantic overtones that later surrounded the tune. Several years later, Isham Jones, who led a well-known orchestra of the times, recorded the first really popular version, though it too was played much faster than singers began to treat it starting in 1929, after Mitchell Parish had supplied a set of lyrics.

Some songs have romantic stories connected with their conception. Not so "Star Dust." "It was very simple," Parish recently explained. "Hoagy and I

Artie!

were both just starting out. We were working as staff writers for Mills Music, but writing separately. One day Hoagy dug out 'Star Dust' and somebody asked me to write lyrics to his melody. I had a job to do, and, as a professional, I did it."

As Parish points out, the song's popularity built gradually. "It was not an overnight hit, and that may account for its longevity," he muses. He also figures, according to estimates by Mills Music, that the song has been recorded approximately one thousand times!

The most lasting of all those recordings, and one which Parish agrees is one of its best, has been the 1940 Artie Shaw version, which, according to Shaw, was sketched by him and orchestrated by Lennie Hayton. It featured Shaw's new string section, and two sensational solos—one by trumpeter Billy Butterfield, the other by trombonist Jack Jenney—that helped to make this the all-time top-selling recording of "Star Dust." Shaw also has pointed out that originally RCA Victor had planned to back his recorded version with one by Tommy Dorsey, but that Dorsey was so overwhelmed by the Shaw rendition that he shied away from the coupling.

While recognizing the Shaw recording as a masterpiece, Parish says his favorite version of all is Nat "King" Cole's, arranged by Gordon Jenkins. "Let me tell you something about this one. When Nat opened at the Copacabana in New York, I was there with Walter Winchell. Now, you know Winchell was supposed to have been a pretty hard-boiled guy. But when Nat started singing 'Star Dust,' tears began pouring down Winchell's cheeks."

Parish credits Winchell for some of the song's enduring popularity. "He just loved it, and he was always plugging it in his column, especially that line, 'When our love was new, and each kiss an inspiration.' "

Today, the two composers of "Star Dust" live three thousand miles apart—Carmichael in California, Parish in New York—and there's a good chance they'll never get together again. Each has written dozens of more hits, but always with different writers, which leads one to believe that "Star Dust" was just one of those freak coincidences that happened to make millionaires out of two guys who just happened to be in the right place at the right time.

As for Shaw, he also lives in California. He hasn't played his clarinet for twenty years, yet he remains creative and productive as an author and producer, specializing in motion pictures and the theater. And he remains busy depositing large royalty checks for his many hit recordings, including, of course, "Star Dust."

Star Dust

Words by MITCHELL PARISH
Music by HOAGY CARMICHAEL

'Tain't What You Do

For sheer rhythmic exuberance and contagious musical fun there was never a band like Jimmie Lunceford's. To give you an idea of how it stacked up against all the rest, take what happened at the greatest big band marathon of all time: twenty-eight bands at an eight-hour session in New York's Manhattan Center on the night of November 18, 1940—a huge musicians' benefit that attracted six thousand enthusiastic fans.

Each band was scheduled to play for fifteen minutes, and all except one did—Benny Goodman, Count Basie, Glenn Miller, Les Brown, Guy Lombardo, Glen Gray, Will Bradley, Sammy Kaye and all the rest. But the one band that didn't, because it couldn't get off the stage in its allotted time, simply because it created such stupendous excitement that the roaring crowd wouldn't let up until it played some more of its romping, stomping numbers, was Jimmie Lunceford's.

This was a band of guys who really loved one another and whose love of each other and the swinging sounds they played was projected with completely uninhibited and fantastically infectious enthusiasm.

One of its most famous numbers, and one which broke it wide open that night, was " 'Tain't What You Do." Sy Oliver, whose seemingly relaxed yet actually hard-driving arrangements set the band's style, wrote the tune. But, he readily admits, the idea was not his:

"Trummy Young [the band's singing trombonist] and I used to room together on the road, and after the gig Trummy used to go out and find himself some session and just jam. Then at five in the morning he'd return to our hotel room—he was a real enthusiastic cat—and sometimes he'd wake me up with an idea for an arrangement or something. Usually, though, I'd just turn over and go back to sleep.

"Well, this one night Trummy comes back and wakes me and tells me he's got a wonderful idea for a song—that he'd been singing the phrase all evening and he wanted me to write a whole tune around it. The way he said it was ' 'Tain't What Ya Do, Hit's the Way Hotcha Do It.' I must say it was one of his better five A.M. ideas, and so I wrote down the title on a sheet of paper and later stuck it in my briefcase and forgot about it.

"One day when we were off, I was sitting on the front porch of a rooming house in Knoxville, Tennessee, and I began rummaging through my case. I

The Lunceford vocal quartet, with Trummy Young second from left.

The great Lunceford band.

came across the title, and it really hit me, so I called Trummy, and that very afternoon we sat down and worked it out, and then I wrote the arrangement and brought it into the band."

On January 3, 1939, the Lunceford band, which hadn't had a recording session in nine months, waxed " 'Tain't What You Do" on its first recording date for Vocalion. It turned out to be one of the band's biggest hits. But no matter how hard he tried, Trummy Young, who sang the vocal on the record, could never again come up with such a great idea at five o'clock in the morning.

'Tain't What You Do
(It's the Way That Cha Do It)

Words and Music by SY OLIVER and
JAMES YOUNG

Tangerine

♩♩♩

"That's a funny name for a song and a girl, isn't it," remarked Bob Eberly, who sang the first chorus on Jimmy Dorsey's famous recording of "Tangerine." "It sounds almost like a gag. They could have called it 'Orange' or 'Persimmon' or even 'Kumquat.' "

But it's easier to rhyme with "tangerine" than with those other fruits, which may be why Johnny Mercer, who wrote the lyrics to this very popular song from the movie *The Fleet's In,* barked up that particular citrus tree. The melody was written by Victor Schertzinger, who directed this film, which starred the Dorsey band along with Dorothy Lamour, Betty Hutton, William Holden and Eddie Bracken. Mercer, of course, has long been recognized as one of the great lyricists of all time, but few realize that Schertzinger, whom Eberly recalls as "a great guy and a typical Hollywood director," also wrote melodies like "Tangerine," "Marcheta," "One Night of Love," "I Remember You" and "Arthur Murray Taught Me Dancing in a Hurry."

"Tangerine" was the fourth of a quartet of Dorsey, three-part hit recordings that included "Amapola," "Yours" and "Green Eyes." Bob would sing the first chorus slowly, as a ballad, then Jimmy would come in at a much brighter tempo for a jazz-styled instrumental passage, after which the band would slow down a bit to allow Helen O'Connell to punch out the final chorus in her own cutesy style.

According to Eberly, the routine was born of necessity. "We were doing a radio series for 20 Grand cigarettes, one of several dime-a-package brands, and the band was being given only three minutes to show what it could do. So Jimmy and Tutti Camarata, who was arranging for us then, came up with the idea of getting all three of us into one arrangement. It worked great on the show, but Decca Records was pretty worried about all those tempo changes. They hadn't been done before on records, so they weren't sure the records would sell. And maybe they thought they might be sued by somebody breaking a leg trying to follow all those tempo changes. Anyway, they let us do it, nobody busted a leg, and, as you know, these became the band's biggest hits."

They also brought Eberly and O'Connell into the spotlight as America's favorite singing couple. Their personal relationship was equally attractive. According to Eberly, "It could have made the perfect setting for one of those

Bob and Helen cut their tangerine cream cake.

happy family TV situation series, the way Helen and I would kid and tease each other while Jimmy guided and watched over us." To this day, they remain very good friends, still appearing together on dates, still bantering and kidding each other. Some members of the band were dead certain there was more to their relationship than appeared on the bandstand, that they were deeply in love and would get married. They were only partially correct; each eventually married someone else, but fewer personal relationships between artists have endured as long and as well as that between the two singers who sang those lyrics that rhyme with "Tangerine" and not with "Kumquat."

P.S. Johnny Mercer, contacted at his California home, insists that no other fruit ever entered his lyric orchard; it was "tangerine" all the way. "When I was just a young kid, I saw a musical show called *Tangerine*. There was no song in it by that name, but the title must have stayed with me because the minute that Victor Schertzinger played his song for me, that title hit me."

Tangerine

by JOHNNY MERCER and VICTOR SCHERTZINGER
From the Paramount Picture "The Fleet's In"

Tenderly

ᴅᴅᴅ

One of the pleasantest places to hang out in the mid-forties was Billy Reed's Little Club in New York's east fifties. There you could hear Doris Day on her first solo appearance and also a great studio pianist named Walter Gross, who would tell his friends, "Hey, I've just written a song I'd like you to hear." And from his piano would come the lovely strains of "Tenderly."

For quite some time, only Gross's fans heard the song. But gradually the word spread around the musical fraternity, and soon it became a favorite not only among singers but among instrumentalists as well.

Trumpeters especially seemed to be attracted, perhaps because it gave them a chance to show off their range. Charlie Spivak and Ray Anthony recorded it, but the most memorable performance was turned in by Randy Brooks, a trumpeter with a brilliant sound that had sparked the bands of Hal Kemp and Les Brown before Randy formed his own group in 1945.

The Brooks band was a musical one. It featured progressive arrangements by John Benson Brooks (no relation) and a bright, new, young tenor saxist

Randy.

named Stan Getz. Off the stand, Randy, built like a guard on a football team, was a charming, down-home type from the state of Maine. On the stand, however, he grew intense, appearing fretful, pouring out all his almost superhuman energies through his sizzling trumpet. He married another bandleader, the very bright and pretty Ina Ray Hutton, and they moved to the West Coast. There he suffered a stroke that finished him as a trumpeter. Dejected and eventually divorced, he returned to Maine, where he died in 1967.

Tenderly

Lyric by JACK LAWRENCE
Music by WALTER GROSS

Valse moderato

The eve-ning breeze ca-ressed the trees ten-der-ly; ___ The tremb-ling trees em-braced the breeze ten-der-ly. ___ Then you and I came wan-der-ing by And lost in a sigh were

There! I've Said It Again

♪♪♪

Sometimes it took a special interpretation by a specialized performer to turn a song into a hit. Such certainly was the case with "There! I've Said It Again."

According to its composer, Dave Mann, former pianist with Jimmy Dorsey, Charlie Spivak, Ray Noble and Artie Shaw and now head of the music department at New York's posh Walden School, recordings of the song by Les Brown with a Doris Day vocal, and by Nat "King" Cole and Benny Carter had made little or no impression at all on the public—so little, in fact, that when its lyricist, Redd Evans, asked for the return of the song from its original publisher, he got it right back.

"Redd was a very aggressive man," according to Mann, "and he always seemed to have a lot of faith in our song, ever since it had germinated sort of spontaneously one day while we were together. He knew Eli Oberstein, the head man at Victor, so after he got the tune back from the publisher, he began plugging it himself. He kept after Eli until he finally assigned it to Vaughn Monroe's band.

"Now, nobody really expected too much of the song. Victor put it on the back side of 'Rum and Coca-Cola,' which was then a big hit because of the Andrews Sisters' record. But then a crazy thing happened. Somebody down in the islands began suing the American composers, claiming they'd stolen the song, and so people started shying away from the tune. And, besides, Vaughn's rendition hadn't made much of an impression.

"In those days, the juke-box operators would buy a lot of records. So here they were stuck with Vaughn's 'Rum and Coca-Cola,' and just so their investment shouldn't be a total loss, they decided to turn the record over and play the other side. And soon everybody, it seems, began putting in nickels to hear Vaughn sing 'There! I've Said It Again.' "

Just how successful was the record? "All I know is that I'd been in the army only a few months when my wife came down to visit me. She had the first royalty check from the record. It was for eighteen thousand dollars and something!"

Monroe must have been equally happy. Though he had studied singing and trumpeting seriously, and took them both that way, he soon became just as serious about commercial success. "The band business," he once insisted,

[299]

"There! I've Said It Again."

"isn't an artistic thing. It's a business. I could name four or five bands that aren't doing well today because they don't do what people ask for." Which is probably precisely why Vaughn Monroe for the rest of his career never stopped singing "There! I've Said It Again."

There! I've Said It Again

Words and Music by REDD EVANS and
DAVE MANN

There Is No Greater Love

There were few sounds among the big bands as rich and warm and melodic as those produced by the Isham Jones orchestra. Throughout its career, from the mid-twenties to the late thirties, its style emphasized a broad, sweeping, rich, round-toned ensemble that other bands tried, with little success, to imitate.

Jones, a tall, scowling, very reserved man, really didn't communicate too well on a personal level with either his audiences—which could account for his never reaching the top of the popularity polls—or with his musicians, most of whom were in awe of him. But he knew exactly how to extract the maximum not just from musicians but from musical notes as well.

For Isham was also an outstanding composer. He wrote a whole gang of hits, including "I'll See You in My Dreams," "It Had to Be You," "The One I Love Belongs to Somebody Else," "On the Alamo," "Swingin' Down the Lane," and one of the most emotional of all ballads, "There Is No Greater Love."

He had in his band two excellent vocalists. Eddie Stone sang the rhythm tunes, and the slim young saxist who emoted ballads, like "There Is No Greater Love," was Woody Herman. In 1936, when some of the Jones musicians decided to form their own cooperative group, they picked Woody as their front man, and that was the start of the Herman Herd.

The Jones band also had two outstanding arrangers and composers, Joe Bishop, later a Herman bandsman, who wrote its famous "Woodchoppers' Ball" and its theme, "Blue Flame," and Gordon Jenkins, who composed Benny Goodman's closing theme, "Goodbye." Later a successful free-lance arranger and conductor (he was Frank Sinatra's musical director), Jenkins had left the Jones band in the mid-thirties with some obvious regrets and some beautiful remembrances, which he revealed in an article he wrote for a 1937 issue of *Metronome* magazine, part of which put the Jones band into an interesting perspective:

> The other night I spent a few hours at the radio, listening to dance bands. I heard 458 chromatic runs on accordions, 911 "telegraph ticker" brass figures, 78 sliding trombones, 4 sliding violas, 45 burps into a straw, 91 bands that played the same arrangement on every tune, and 11,006 imitations of Benny Goodman.

The Isham Jones band.

These figures are slightly exaggerated, but that was my personal impression. Slightly nauseated, I went to bed, and lay for some time thinking about the "good old days" and the old Jones band. There, gents, was a band . . . probably the greatest sweet ensemble of that time, or any other time. Believe me, when I say that writing for that band was fun, not work.

There Is No Greater Love

Words by MARTY SYMES
Music by ISHAM JONES

There's a Small Hotel

♩ ♩ ♩

Some of the lushest sounds of the big band era were played by an orchestra that also gave out with some of the most modern jazz arrangements—Claude Thornhill's. No other band, with the possible exception of Tommy Dorsey's, could offer such diversity with so much finesse. Its ability to create moods, both sentimental and exhilarating, was indeed a joy to hear.

Its ballad sound was absolutely gorgeous, with French horns and various reeds mixed in with a brass choir that employed a wide range of voicings and dynamics. Claude's choice of songs was exquisite, and one of his favorites was a Rodgers and Hart tune called "There's a Small Hotel," which had originally been written for a 1935 show called *Jumbo*, yanked at the last minute, and then introduced the following year in another of their Broadway musicals, *On Your Toes*. In addition to the full-bodied reeds and ensemble, the Thornhill recording also featured a delicate-sounding vocal group called "The Snowflakes," an amusing name, since Claude was considered by many to have been quite flaky himself.

Actually, Thornhill was much more than that. He was vague, but he was also warm and charming, and an immensely talented pianist and arranger. He had studied at the Cincinnati Conservatory and the Curtis Institute in Philadelphia, and had worked with all of New York's top studio musicians during the early thirties, as well as in the bands of Hal Kemp, Ray Noble, Benny Goodman and Andre Kostelanetz, for whom he also arranged.

He formed his band in 1939 on the West Coast, but it took him until the summer of 1941, when it played at the Glen Island Casino, to gain recognition. Its music reflected much of Claude's personality. It was gentle yet virile, soft yet strong, subtle yet bright, witty yet profound, warm yet cool.

The warmth permeated the ballads, arranged by Claude, Bill Borden and a young Gil Evans. The cool came through in the jazz, where Evans, who, by the way, wrote the Thornhill arrangement of "There's a Small Hotel," introduced the sort of modern voicings that he later utilized in his famous scores for Miles Davis.

Claude was a kind man and a generous man, who constantly encouraged his compatriots to broaden their musical horizons. Few leaders or musicians ever earned so much respect. Modern jazz pianist Thelonious Monk once called Thornhill's "the only really good big band I've heard in years." And

"I wish that we were there . . . together."

when Claude died suddenly in the summer of 1965, his widow received a call from Duke Ellington. "I wonder," he told her, "if the world will ever know how much it had in this beautiful man. He never wanted anything from anybody. If he called you, he just called to talk—or else he might want to give *you* something. You know, there aren't many of his kind left. . . . Yes, he was a beautiful man."

There's a Small Hotel

Lyric by LORENZ HART
Music by RICHARD RODGERS

Moderately

There's a small ho - tel With a wish - ing well; I wish that we were there to - geth - er. There's a

This Love of Mine

Some of the most tender and poignant sounds of the big band era emerged on recordings that Frank Sinatra made with the Tommy Dorsey band. Played softly and intimately, at a slower tempo than other bands recorded, they featured Tommy's muted trombone and what the writers liked to refer to as "Sinatra's swooning crooning style."

One performance that typifies exquisitely the blending of their talents is their rendition of "This Love of Mine," written by Sinatra, Sol Parker and Hank Sanicola, who later was to become Frank's personal manager. Its relaxed me-to-you manner reflects wonderfully the musical ambiance that had developed between the young singer and the leader whom Sinatra has always graciously credited with helping him develop his style. "Even without lyrics," he once pointed out, "Tommy made it sound so musical that you never lost the thread of the message."

In addition to admiring Dorsey's musicianship—Frank was especially fascinated by Tommy's breath control and tried to emulate that process—the young singer also looked up to his leader personally. Actually, the two were very much alike: headstrong, volatile, musical perfectionists, kooky senses of humor, high livers—and yet beneath it all, gentle, sentimental and caring.

It took a while for Tommy to fully appreciate the talents of "the kid" whom he had snatched from the Harry James band. But the more songs Frank sang, and the deeper the sighs of the young girls who came to listen and gawk, the more Tommy began to realize that he didn't have just another band singer in his midst. And so he began to build arrangements around Frank, encouraging his young singer, and establishing him, along with his own trombone, as one of his band's vital organs.

For a while, these two strong personalities hit it off famously. But there was one other trait they shared: ambition. Thus, in the summer of 1942, after two and half years with the band, and with no blessings whatsoever from his suddenly disillusioned and disappointed leader, Sinatra pulled out to begin his fabulous career as a single performer. And right then and there, one of the finest eras in the history of one of the greatest of all the big bands drew to a close.

TD and FS.

This Love of Mine

Words by FRANK SINATRA
Music by SOL PARKER and HENRY SANICOLA

To Each His Own

♪♪♪

Eddy Howard emerged as one of the country's most popular bandleaders in 1946, just as the big band era was drawing to a close. The reason: his hit recording of "To Each His Own," a gentle ballad, sung intimately and sentimentally by this soft-spoken, relaxed former guitarist and vocalist with the Dick Jurgens band.

Before organizing his own band, Howard had been on the singing scene for almost a generation, beginning with a stint on a Los Angeles radio station while still in his teens, then graduating to the bands of Eddie Fitzpatrick, Tom Gerun (Woody Herman, Tony Martin and Ginny Sims also worked for Gerun), Ben Bernie and finally Jurgens. With Dick's band he recorded two hits, "My Last Good-bye" and "Careless," before leaving in 1940 to work as a single in clubs and on records.

A man of exquisite musical taste (his singing was always gentle and relaxed), Howard employed such musical greats as Teddy Wilson and Charlie Christian on his recordings. Then, in 1941, he organized his own band. Smaller than most groups of the era and sticking closely to pretty sounds, it

Eddy

[319]

was only moderately successful until he recorded his top-selling version of "To Each His Own."

The song was written by Jay Livingston and Ray Evans, a prolific team, formed when the two undergraduates met at the University of Pennsylvania. Together they composed scores for more than three dozen movies (in 1949 they wrote for seven in just that one year!) and a couple of Broadway musicals.

Following the success of "To Each His Own," and the decline of the big bands, Eddy was able to keep his smaller band working because (1) its payroll was less than those of most bands and (2) his was a singer-oriented unit that fit easily into the new era of singers. But ill health eventually forced him to disband, and he died in 1963 in Palm Desert, California.

To Each His Own

by JAY LIVINGSTON
and RAY EVANS

Undecided

One of the big bands' favorite tunes came out of one of the best of the small bands: John Kirby's. This was a slick six-piece unit, led by Chick Webb's former bassist, that played light, delicate swing. It featured arrangements and an occasional original by its elegant trumpeter, Charlie Shavers. One of those originals, "Undecided," turned out to be the group's most successful number.

The tune has been a favorite among musicians ever since the Kirby band's recording of 1938. It's one of those songs that seems to swing by itself, and it has been recorded many times by jazz groups, including a memorable rendition a few years ago by Benny Goodman's septet when it was playing in New York's Rainbow Grill.

The big bands loved to play the tune also. Goodman had a fine arrangement for his fourteen-piece outfit, but probably the most exciting was Red Norvo's. I can still remember one night driving leisurely through North Carolina and picking up the Norvo band's broadcast from Murray's in Tuckahoe, New York, and hearing it just build and build and build for around fifteen minutes on the tune's simple, swinging riff. It got me so excited that by the time the band had finished I was shocked to find that I'd been trying

The John Kirby band with Kirby on bass, composer Charlie Shavers on trumpet, pianist Billy Kyle, Jr., clarinetist Buster Bailey, saxist Russell Procope and drummer O'Neill Spencer.

to keep pace with the band's buildup and was doing around seventy miles an hour—quite a scary speed for North Carolina roads of the thirties.

The song can also be a singer's delight, and nobody has turned in a more invigorating recording than Ella Fitzgerald, when she was still a member of Chick Webb's band. Those were the days when she still had that little-girl approach to her jazz, and the way she intoned the words "What are you g-o-i-n-g to do" still sounds like the classic complaint of a frustrated, thwarted teen-ager.

The Kirby band, because of its gentle approach to jazz, was invited to play engagements usually reserved for white groups—like New York's Waldorf-Astoria—and a network radio series that also featured Kirby's wife, Maxine Sullivan. After the sextet disbanded in the early forties, Shavers embarked on an instrumental career that found him featured in the bands of Goodman, Raymond Scott and Tommy Dorsey. He died July 8, 1971, just two days after the passing of his all-time idol, Louis Armstrong.

Undecided

Words by SID ROBIN
Music by CHARLES SHAVERS

First you say you do and then you don't, and then you say you will and then you won't._ You're un-de-cid-ed now, so what are you gon-na do?_ Now you want to play, and

Until the Real Thing Comes Along

♩♩♩

"There were these three kids from Topeka, Kansas—I can't even remember their names—who used to come down to Kansas City in the late twenties where we and a lot of other bands were playing," recalls Andy Kirk, whose band in 1936 recorded the big hit version of "Until the Real Thing Comes Along." "They used to sing in the various clubs and they'd feature a number they called 'The Slave Song.' Everybody played it. But nobody ever recorded it."

In 1929 the Kirk band made its first records. But, as Kirk points out, "they were what we used to call race records—just for the colored trade. Jack Kapp would come out to Kansas City from New York for Brunswick Records and they'd set us up in the studios of station WDAF, and we'd just sit there and jam." Almost invariably the results turned out to be a mixture of jazz and early rhythm and blues. "But then, in the mid-thirties, Jack started his own label, Decca Records, and he sent for us to come to New York to record."

Again, Kapp sought a batch of "race records." But Kirk, whose band had become more sophisticated by then, and was now featuring a slick ballad singer named Pha Terrell, wanted to get out of the rut. "I told Jack about 'The Slave Song,' which Pha was singing with us, but he just said, 'Look, every time you guys have something good going, you want to do what the white boys are doing.' " So Kirk, a very persuasive, softspoken gent explained the facts of black band life to Kapp, emphasizing that when they played for black dancers, they included a number of ballads. Finally Kapp agreed to let Kirk record his ballad.

"The first time we recorded it, we did it as 'The Slave Song.' But Jack refused to release it because he didn't like the lyrics. So he called in two young songwriters who had just started out, Sammy Cahn and Saul Chaplin, and had them fix up the song. They gave it the title 'Until the Real Thing Comes Along,' we recorded it again, and it became a big hit."

Nevertheless, Kirk, one of the best liked and most gracious bandleaders, continued to play jazz. His band often featured the piano, arrangements and composition of the great Mary Lou Williams, much to the delight of jazz aficionados the world over. And yet, despite his band's great contributions to jazz, Andy Kirk still is remembered most for "Until the Real Thing Comes Along."

Leader Andy Kirk, singer Pha Terrell and pianist-arranger-composer Mary Lou Williams.

Until the Real Thing Comes Along

Words and Music by MANN HOLINER, ALBERTA NICHOLS, SAMMY CAHN, SAUL CHAPLIN and L. E. FREEMAN

When It's Sleepy Time
Down South

♪♪♪

One of the most evocative of all theme songs for years heralded the appearance of one of the few true superstars of American music—the great Louis Armstrong. Whether it was on radio or television or at any of America's Ambassador of Good Will's thousands of personal appearances in countries all over the world, "When It's Sleepy Time Down South" set the stage and the mood for some of the warmest, most thrilling sounds of all time.

Armstrong, the New Orleans waif who achieved stardom through his horn, his gravel voice and his showmanship, could turn any tune that his trumpet touched into a musical gem. And when he dug into one as emotional in itself as "When It's Sleepy Time Down South," the results would be absolutely magnificent.

"Pale moon shinin' on the fields below. . . ."

Pops on a radio show with Jerry Lewis, Dean Martin, Bob Hope, Meredith Willson, Frankie Laine, Tallulah Bankhead and Deborah Kerr.

Louis first recorded the song on the Okeh label back in 1931, a year after it had been written and its composers, Leon and Otis René and Clarence Muse, had brought it to him to play. "That first version was always Louis's favorite," points out his widow, Lucille. "He recorded it many times after that, but that remained the one he liked best." Mrs. Armstrong also reveals that it took a number of years before Louis selected the song as his theme. "By then it had become such a big hit and so identified with him that he decided he should use it as his theme."

The impact of Armstrong's creativity and style upon music and musicians cannot possibly be overestimated. Some years ago, when Harry James learned that he had won an important trumpet poll, he reacted candidly and a bit emotionally: "That's ridiculous. How could anybody else win that poll when Louis is still alive!"

Idolized as he was by musicians and fans all over the world, and entertained and feted regally by royalty in so many exotic lands, Armstrong nevertheless continued to live a simple life in his home in Queens, just across the river from busy Manhattan. Those who knew him must have wondered sometimes whether he ever fully appreciated his contributions to the big wide world that he loved so much. For he remained, until his death at the age of seventy-one in 1971, a man with great pride but seemingly no vanity at all.

Perhaps his feelings about his music and himself are best illustrated by his reaction to a request he received during the sixties after one of his fabulously successful appearances: "There was this little girl after the concert who came up to me and asked me for my autograph and I gave it to her and the next thing I heard her screaming, 'Gee, he touched my hand!' Let's face it. I was in my sixties then. So it's not me that gets her excited. It's got to be my music!"

When It's Sleepy Time Down South

Words and Music by LEON RENÉ, OTIS RENÉ
and CLARENCE MUSE

Slowly, with a beat

Pale moon shin-ing on the fields be - low,__ Folks are croon-ing songs soft and low,__ Need - n't tell me so, be-cause I know__ it's sleep-y time down south. Soft winds blow-ing thru the

When My Baby Smiles at Me

♩♩♩

"The High Hat Tragedian of Song" is what they used to call Ted Lewis, because, happy as he may have seemed as a performer (his favorite expression was "Is everybody happy?"), his downward inflections made almost everything he sang sound as though doomsday were just around the corner.

"When My Baby Smiles at Me" was his theme song, and to emphasize Lewis' approach to a song, during his rendition the horns in his band used to gliss downward at almost every open spot. Thus, though this is basically a very happy sounding song with a joyous message, the Lewis treatment still managed to inject some semblance of tragedy.

Lewis, born Theodore Leopold Friedman, grew up during the vaudeville days, eventually leaving the boards to organize and front a very good dance

"Is everybody happy?"

band that from time to time included Benny Goodman, Jimmy Dorsey, Fats Waller, Muggsy Spanier and other jazz notables. Lewis himself played a corny clarinet, but when he blew into it, with his beat-up top hat perched at an angle upon his head, the crowds would go wild.

Singing—or rather, half-singing and half-talking—was his forte, however. He introduced "When My Baby Smiles at Me" in his semi-something style all the way back in 1918 at Rector's Cafe in New York, and he was still getting so many requests for it that he featured it in his final New York nightclub appearance forty-seven years later!

They may have called him a tragedian. Yet Lewis, like a true vaudevillian trouper, seemed to be dedicated to making everybody happy. Or else why was he always asking the same question?

When My Baby Smiles at Me

Words and Music by HARRY VON TILZER, ANDREW
B. STERLING, BILL MUNRO and TED LEWIS

Who Wouldn't Love You

♩♩♩

Kay Kyser sent word from the Christian Science Center in Boston, where he now heads the film and broadcasting department, that he really doesn't remember any details about his recording of "Who Wouldn't Love You," a tune written by Bill Carey and the late Carl Fischer, who also composed the gorgeous "You've Changed." But, despite Kay's lack of even semi-total recall, millions of Americans still do remember, with a good deal of nostalgia, the Kyser band's big 1942 hit that featured the homey singing and whistling of Harry Babbitt and Trudy Erwin, and those catchy rim shots on a snare drum.

Kyser led a tremendously popular band. Its music was seldom—at least during its early years—especially distinctive or outstanding, so Kay, a very smart and shrewd businessman, concentrated on other attention-getting devices. The first of these was his singing-song-title gambit in which one of his vocalists would sing the name of the song at the start of each arrangement. Another, and even more successful, was Kay Kyser's College of Musical Knowledge, a song-guessing game with prizes for the winning participants. Kyser initiated the idea when he was playing in Chicago's Blackhawk Restaurant in 1934; eventually it became so popular that it evolved into a local radio show and finally into a national network series that lasted for many years.

In the beginning, Kyser's band was strictly in the Mickey Mouse class, complete with simpering saxes and ricky-tick trumpets. But in later years, it developed into an outstanding musical outfit, with smart, updated arrangements played by some of the best available musicians.

Throughout a career that covered recordings, radio, television and movies (Kay had become quite a personality by then), Kyser placed much emphasis on his vocalists, including two novelty singers, "Ish Kabibble," really Merwyn Bogue, a good trumpeter turned comedian, and Sully Mason, who also played sax. On ballads, he featured several girls, including the attractive Ginny Sims, whom he reportedly almost married, and the very beautiful, intelligent Georgia Carroll, whom he did marry. Among the boy ballad singers, Babbitt was the best known, though in the late forties a youngster named Michael Douglas, who later became *the* Mike Douglas, turned in some good recorded sides along with a group called The Campus Kids.

Kyser's bandleading career had begun on the campus of the University of

Vocalist Babbitt and maestro Kyser.

"Who wouldn't love you-all?"

North Carolina. Once destined to become a lawyer, he succeeded in maintaining an objectivity regarding his career and the world around him that would have benefited other leaders who were unable to retire as comfortably as he did. As one of his associates once described him, "He is a man of contradictions and extremes. On the bandstand he can be the soul of dignity and buffoonery, either one. But off the bandstand Kay is a practical but shrewd businessman [he reportedly grossed a million dollars in just one year], an unassuming person leading a normal life of clean habits and simple tastes."

His habits and tastes eventually took him away from the band business and into a life strongly devoted to religion. He returned to his home state of North Carolina, where for years he and his wife dedicated themselves to Christian Science. In 1974, they moved to the sect's headquarters in Boston, where Kay immersed himself in a life of teaching and of spreading the faith with undoubtedly just as much zeal and devotion as he had used to create and maintain one of the most successful dance bands of all time.

Who Wouldn't Love You

Words by BILL CAREY
Music by CARL FISCHER

Why Don't We Do This More Often

One of the more delightful vocalists of the big band era was impish-looking-and-sounding Eddie Stone, who, when he sang anything bordering on the romantic, gave out with an "I'm-sorta-kidding-but-then-again-maybe-I'm-not-but-why-don't-you-take-me-a-little-bit-seriously-anyway" approach. His major band career began with the Isham Jones band during the late twenties, and it climaxed when he made a couple of hit records with Freddy Martin's band in the early forties.

Eddie's two most important vocals were on Martin's versions of "The Hut Sut Song" and a tune that seemed to have been made to order for his style,

Leader Martin (with sax) and vocalist Stone (left, with fiddle).

"Why Don't We Do This More Often." Written by two veteran songwriters, Allie Wrubel and Charles Newman, it appeared on the back side of Freddy's most successful record, "Tonight We Love," based on Tchaïkovsky's Piano Concerto. According to Martin, when Wrubel and Newman heard that their song was going to be paired with "some classical piece," they objected strenuously. "Who'd ever buy a piece of classical music played by a dance band?" they asked. "We will!" figuratively replied over a million record buyers, as they plunked down their seventy-five cents.

For years, Martin had led one of the better dance bands that played primarily pretty and always danceable music. He always had good singers, some with funny names like Elmer Feldkamp, and some who would become famous, like Helen Ward, after she joined Benny Goodman, and a young and then chubby pianist/singer named Merv Griffin, who became famous all by himself.

Martin, tremendously well liked by his fellow bandleaders, always enjoyed his work, and, during the seventies, proved it when he revived some of the big band sounds via "The Big Band Cavalcade" coast-to-coast series of one-night stands in concert halls and ballrooms (Bob Crosby, Frankie Carle, Art Mooney and Buddy Morrow also participated), which brought back many fond memories and also introduced his kind of music to a younger and often quite intrigued generation.

Why Don't We Do This More Often

Lyric by CHARLES NEWMAN
Music by ALLIE WRUBEL

Why Don't You Do Right

♪♪♪

When Peggy Lee was singing in theaters with Benny Goodman's band, she naturally spent a good deal of time in her dressing room. There she would listen to records on her wind-up portable, which she fondly called "my road-runner phonograph. I had a strange collection of records. There was Laura Newell playing Ravel. And there was something by Debussy, and 'Valse Triste.' And eventually I even got to 'Swan Lake.' "

But mixed in with these was Peggy's favorite, a record by a black singer unknown to the general public but deservedly admired by anyone who was into the blues. Her name: Lil Green. Her song: "Why Don't You Do Right," written by a little-known blues composer named Joe McCoy.

"Benny used to hear me playing it all the time, and so one day he came into my room and he said, 'You really like that, don't you?' I was rather shy and unsure then, so I asked him if it bothered him. He said, 'Oh, no, but how would you like us to make an arrangement of it for you?' Of course I wanted it. And so he did."

The tune was one of the last the Goodman band recorded before the infamous musicians' recording ban of 1942. "As soon as it came out, people began noticing me," Peggy recalls. It became a smash hit, remaining in the number-one spot for quite some time. And it has lasted. "I still include it in my program today," Peggy points out.

A very sensitive and sentimental lady, she was deeply affected by the song's impact on the servicemen overseas during World War II. "They tell me that it traveled through the war from one theater of operations to another." What touched her most of all, however, was the report from her own brother: "He told me that when he was on the boat taking him across the channel during the second wave of the Normandy invasion, they were playing 'Why Don't You Do Right' over the p.a. system to boost the men's morale. What a weird feeling that must have been for him—right in the middle of the invasion—and hearing his own sister singing that song to him!"

"Why Don't You Do Right" and "Somebody Else Is Taking My Place" and "How Long Has This Been Going On" and other recordings all helped to establish Peggy as an important voice with Goodman, who had discovered her working with a trio in a Chicago hotel cocktail lounge. Yet she hadn't im-

Benny, Peggy, pianist Jess Stacy and saxist Hymie Shertzer.

pressed too many people at first. "Maybe we didn't give her the right songs to begin with," Goodman recently mused. "But once she got the right material, she really took off, didn't she!" That she certainly did, to become one of the most musical and successful singers of all time. Extremely astute and aware, she has, more than most ex-band vocalists, kept up with the musical times.

But still, she appreciates her early days. Goodman's kindness impressed her. But so did his legendary absent-mindedness. "I'll never forget the night he asked me to have dinner with him. We got into a cab and we just sat there. Finally the driver turned around to find out where we wanted to go. But Benny just kept sitting there in a sort of fog. Finally I nudged him, and he looked up and saw the driver looking back at him. 'Oh,' he said, 'I'm sorry. Er—er—how much do I owe you?'"

Why Don't You Do Right

Lyrics and Music by JOE McCOY

Yes Indeed!

♩♩♩♩

The Tommy Dorsey band produced not only great ballad records but also some of the swingingest big band sides of all time. One of the big reasons: big, handsome, ebullient arranger, singer, composer Sy Oliver.

Though the Tommy Dorsey band's record made it famous, "Yes Indeed!" had actually been written by Oliver when he had been a member of the Jimmie Lunceford band. "But Jimmie thought it was sacrilegious, so we never played it," Sy recently reported. "There's quite a story connected with that song: In the Lunceford band we had a bass player named Mose Allen. Late at night, when we were riding on our bus, he used to break us up with a takeoff on those holy-roly preachers. He called it 'The Trials and Tribulations of the Children of Israel in the Wilderness,' and for the climax of his tale he'd announce very pompously, 'Finally the children of Israel got to the Flap Jack Tree by the River Molasses and they mopped the ol' son of a bitch dry.'

"Well, we all thought it was so funny that I decided to write an act for Mose when we played the Apollo Theater up in Harlem. It was built around 'Yes Indeed!' But Jimmie wouldn't let us do it—as I said, he thought the song was sacrilegious. So I just forgot it.

"Then about five years later, I was with Tommy [Dorsey] out in Hollywood in Bing Crosby's room listening to a background arrangement of a tune called 'You Lucky People, You,' which Bing was going to record the next day. But obviously he didn't like the arrangement, and before I could stop him, Tommy said, 'Hey, Sy, why don't you knock off an arrangement for Bing!' So I wrote one overnight, and Bing was so pleased that he said he wanted to do something for me in return, like introducing a song of mine on his radio show, 'The Kraft Music Hall.' So I gave him 'Yes Indeed,' and he not only introduced it but he also recorded it with Connee Boswell.

"Now you know that just about everything Bing recorded in those days became a hit record. But not 'Yes Indeed.' Don't ask me why. Anyway, Tommy liked the tune and suggested I fix it up for the big band. We might never have recorded it, but on one of our dates we had about a half hour left on the session, and Tommy knew I always carried a spare arrangement around in my briefcase—just for one of those emergencies. So I dug out 'Yes Indeed.'

"You'll shout when it hits you. . . ."

". . . Yes Indeed!"

"Originally, the entire band was supposed to sing those backgrounds, but the guys, who, after all, weren't singers, didn't have time to get the feel of it.

So I switched the vocal parts around for just Jo Stafford and me. She got it right away. By then, we only had enough time left for one take, but on one take we did it . . . and there it was!"

And there it remained, one of the biggest of all the many Tommy Dorsey hits, and one of the swingingest sides ever to emerge from the big band era.

Yes Indeed!

Words and Music by
SY OLIVER

You're Driving Me Crazy!

♩♩♩

Rudy Vallee and Mel Torme recorded it. So did Bob Crosby and His Bob Cats and also the Hoosier Hot Shots. Even a jazz player as far out as tenor saxist Lester Young played it, regularly. And yet the two most significant recordings of Walter Donaldson's "You're Driving Me Crazy!" were made years earlier, in 1930, when the song first appeared as part of the score of a Broadway musical comedy called *Smiles* that featured Fred and Adele As-

Louis and editor George T. Simon.

taire. And they were made by two of the most disparate bandleaders: Guy Lombardo and Louis Armstrong.

The prolific Donaldson had been writing all sorts of big hits—"At Sundown," "Little White Lies," "Love Me or Leave Me," "Makin' Whoopee," "My Blue Heaven," "My Buddy"—so it wasn't surprising that two recording artists with entirely different styles would latch on to his latest. Even then they were looking for those elusive hit records.

The Lombardo rendition featured a vocal by brother Carmen. The Armstrong version naturally focused on Louis's singing. They couldn't have been more opposite; yet both were extremely effective.

What may come as a surprise, however, to many is the tremendous admiration and respect that Lombardo and Armstrong had for each other's music. Louis could see firsthand the effect of Guy's music on his people. For example, when the Lombardo band played a one-nighter in Harlem's Savoy Ballroom, it broke the spot's all-time attendance record. The band even tried playing jazz with a rendition of "St. Louis Blues" in which Carmen would hold a clarinet note while the band would keep yelling "Hold it, Carmen, hold it!" until Carmen finally let go of the note. It was a good act, though hardly a monumental jazz performance.

On the other hand, what has consistently amazed Armstrong admirers has been his obvious and often-stated love of the tremulous Lombardo sax sound. Louis used to call the Lombardos "my inspirators," because he loved the way the band treated a ballad. He even worked on the saxists in his own band to get them to use the same sort of vibrato that the Lombardos did. To jazz purists it sounded quite ridiculous, those simpering, schmaltzy sounds behind Louis's vital, virile trumpet. But Louis loved it, and, judging from the way he played on his recordings of that era, including "You're Driving Me Crazy!" the Lombardo sax sound could very well have inspired, at least to some degree, this greatest of all great jazz artists.

You're Driving Me Crazy!

Words and Music by
WALTER DONALDSON

Credits

᪣ ᪣ ᪣

The publisher would like to thank the following for permission to use photographs:

Page 2, RCA Records; 7 (above), *Metronome*; 7 (below), *Metronome* (David Hecht); 13, *Down Beat*; 18, Otto Hess; 23, 29, 36, 40, *Metronome*; 41, CBS; 49, *Metronome*; 54 (above), *Metronome* (Bill Mark); 54 (below), Harry James; 58, *Metronome*; 66, Sammy Kaye; 72, *Metronome*; 76, Larry Clinton; 83, 89, CBS; 95, RCA Records; 99 (above), Benny Goodman; 99 (below), Gene Krupa; 103, *Metronome*; 108, Universal Pictures; 112, *Metronome*; 117, Otto Hess; 122, 127, 132, 138, *Metronome*; 142, RCA Records; 147, *Metronome*; 152, RCA Records; 157, Sammy Kaye; 161 (left), *Metronome*; 161 (right), *Metronome* (The Photo Illustrators); 165, *Metronome* (Columbia Records); 170, *Metronome* (Bill Mark); 176, *Metronome*; 180 (above), *Metronome* (Gene Lester); 180 (center and below), *Metronome*; 186, *Metronome* (RKO Radio Pictures); 191, Ed Polic; 196 (above), *Metronome* (Barry Kramer); 196 (below, left), *Metronome* (RCA Records); 196 (below, right), *Metronome*; 200, Dolores O'Neill; 205, CBS; 210, *Metronome*; 214 (above), *Metronome* (Universal Pictures); 214 (below), CBS; 220, *Metronome*; 224, *Metronome* (Otto Hess); 230, RCA Records; 235, CBS; 240, *Metronome* (Jay Seymour); 245, *Down Beat*; 249, *Metronome*; 254, *Metronome* (Photographic Illustrations); 260, CBS; 265, *Metronome*; 269, RCA Records; 275, Decca Records; 279, *Down Beat*; 285 (above), CBS; 285 (below), Jimmie Crawford; 291, 295, 300, *Metronome*; 305, CBS; 310, *Metronome*; 315, RCA Records; 319, 324, *Metronome*; 330, *Down Beat*; 335, *Metronome* (NBC); 340, *Metronome*; 346, Columbia Records; 351, *Metronome*; 356, *Metronome* (Al Hauser); 362 (above), *Metronome*; 362 (below), RCA Records; 366, Bert Block.

About the Author

George T. Simon is acknowledged as the big bands' foremost authority and historian. During his twenty years with *Metronome* magazine, he lived among all the leaders, musicians, arrangers and vocalists, getting to know them and their music on a very personal basis.

Such a close working relationship has resulted in a series of important books about that era: *The Big Bands,* now in its fourth edition and seventeenth printing; the incisive *Glenn Miller and His Orchestra;* the gigantic *Simon Says: The Sights and Sounds of the Swing Era;* two earlier books, *The Feeling of Jazz* and *The Bandleader;* and his most recent work, *The Best of the Music Makers,* which covers an even broader spectrum of popular music.

He has also been involved in big bands as a musician (he played drums in the original Glenn Miller band and is still actively playing), as a songwriter, as a critic (in addition to *Metronome,* he also wrote regularly for the New York *Herald Tribune,* the New York *Sun,* and more recently for the New York *Post*), as a producer of records for many labels, and as producer/writer/consultant for musical television shows on all three networks. Formerly an executive director of the National Academy of Recording Arts and Sciences, which he now serves as a consultant, and member of the Newport Jazz Festival, he resides with his wife, Beverly, right in the heart of his native and favorite city, New York.